Holes
in the
Darkness

Teddy Butler Copeland

Holes

in the

Darkness

Lambert Book House
4139 Parkway Drive
Florence, Alabama 35630

I have in my files numerous items with no point of reference
and whose original usage I was unable to trace. Thus, I extend my apologies for
any illustrations not adequately documented.

Published by
Lambert Book House
4139 Parkway Drive
Florence, Alabama 35630

ISBN 978-0-89315-414-1

Printed in the United States of America

CONTENTS

INTRODUCTION

One evening when Robert Louis Stevenson was just a boy, he stood at dusk by a window in his home, looking out on the street as darkness enveloped the city. This, of course, was in the days before electricity, when communities had lamp posts that had to be hand-lit by torches.

As he stood there, so captivated, someone asked young Stevenson what he saw out the window that intrigued him.

"There is a man coming up the street," he replied, "and he is making holes in the darkness."

Making holes in the darkness. What better description could be given for the task God's people have in the world today?

Darkness of sin engulfs everything around us. We cannot completely make it go away. Yet, as God's lamplighters, we can make a difference.

The purpose of this study is to look at the role of light in God's Word, both Old and New Testaments. We will not only see that God is light, as we're told in 1 John 1:5, but that His Word is light as well. And, in addition to that, He expects His children to shine as lights in a darkened world (Philippians 2:15).

CHAPTER 1

The Darkness Around Us

The Darkness Around Us

In the fall of 2001, I was beginning a new ladies' class on Wednesday evenings in the congregation where I worship. The study was entitled *Holes in the Darkness,* and in the first session, as an introduction to the idea of how desperately Christian light is needed, I planned to discuss the darkness that currently exists in the world.

To illustrate, I pulled from my files an article from the *USA Today* newspaper my husband had brought home several months earlier. "You've got to read this," I remember him saying as he handed me the June 26 issue. "You're not going to believe it."

The front-page article, written by Jack Kelley, was subtitled "The secret world of suicide bombers." Under a bold headline—DEVOTION, DESIRE DRIVE YOUTHS TO 'MARTYRDOM'—it proclaimed "Palestinians in pursuit of paradise turn their own bodies into weapons."

> *"You don't start educating . . . at age 22. You start at kindergarten."*

Appalled, I read a quote from a so-called *terrorism expert* who said, "You do not start educating a *shaheed* (holy martyr) at age 22. You start at kindergarten so by the time he is 22, he is looking for an opportunity to sacrifice his life."

As if to verify the statement, on the inside page I saw a photograph that literally gave me cold chills. Taken by Ali Hashisho, it showed little children dressed as suicide bombers for an anti-Israel parade at a refugee camp in southern Lebanon. As I studied the picture, I could not help but recall parades in which my own children participated when they were young, dressed as some of their heroes (American presidents, police officers, etc.). The look they had in their eyes—which I had found so adorable at the time—was mirrored before me in these little ones from the other side of the world. *This is what I'm going to be when I grow up!* it seemed to say.

Equally disturbing was a quote from an 11-year-old Hamas student: "I will make my body a bomb that will blast the flesh of Zionists, the sons of pigs and monkeys. I will tear their bodies into little pieces and cause them more pain than they will ever know."

Reading on, I continued to shudder at the pride expressed by parents whose sons had killed Israelis, dying themselves in the process. "I am very happy and . . . frankly, a bit jealous," one man stated. "My son has fulfilled the Prophet's (Mohammed's) wishes. He has become a hero! Tell me, what more could a father ask?"

That Wednesday evening in class, I tried to portray to my Christian sisters the reality of something we all found incomprehensible. "Lured by promises of financial stability for their families, eternal martyrdom and unlimited sex in the afterlife," stated Kelly in a section I read aloud, "dozens of militant Palestinians . . . aspire to blow themselves up. Their goal: to kill or injure as many Jews as possible in the hope that Israel will withdraw from Gaza and the West Bank."

We all shook our heads that night, I recall, sufficiently horrified. And yet, subconsciously perhaps, I think we were comforted by the realization that, after all, this atrocity was taking place on a continent far away, in a culture we could not even begin to understand, even if we'd tried. *At least it is not happening here*, we thought, squelching any overt concerns.

By the time our class met a second time, however, all of that had changed. Ironically, just days after our discussion of suicide bombers had taken place, those things we had found difficult to even fathom had been played out right before our very eyes. On September 11, Middle Eastern pilots took over four U.S. planes and purposefully crashed them, resulting in the destruction of New York City's World Trade Center towers and the loss of thousands of lives.

It was the darkest time that most people of my generation had ever experienced.

What does Proverbs 22:6 teach about the significance of training in early years?

_____

_____

_____

_____

_____

COMPARISONS TO PEARL HARBOR

Having been born on December 7, I was more than familiar with the infamous Japanese attack that had eventually led to World War II, even though it occurred thirteen years before my actual birth.

All of my life, whenever I would state my birth date, without fail, people older than me always responded, "That's Pearl Harbor day."

It was automatic, something I had come to expect. Yet I must admit, I never fully understood the significant emotional attachment people had to that event. Never, that is, until the fall of 2001.

Since then, however, I understand precisely. Anytime I hear a reference, however casual, to the date "September 11," I have a similar response.

The day the towers fell is etched into our national consciousness, just as the surprise attack on U.S. troops in Hawaii made an indelible impression on the people of my parents' generation.

"Two very *dark* days in the history of our country," newscasters said repeatedly as they compared the events.

Dark indeed.

What memories do you have of September 11, 2001?

_____

_____

_____

TIMES OF DARKNESS IN THE BIBLE

"Darkness" is defined by Webster as *absence of light* or *lack of illumination*. Often it is a symbol for gloom or despair. Throughout the pages of the Bible, we can note several occasions when darkness prevailed.

The first is in the beginning of time. Genesis 1:2 tells us that before God's creation began, *"the earth was formless and empty, darkness was over the surface of the deep."*

Darkness then, as so often is still the case today, was associated with chaos, disorder, confusion. All of that, of course, changed with the speaking of God's simple command: *"Let there be light."*

Another instance of darkness is found in Exodus 10. The ninth plague brought upon the Egyptians—surpassed in consternation only by the tenth and final, the death of the firstborn—was a murkiness that lasted for three long days. "No one could see anyone else or leave his place" is how the Bible describes a darkness so intense that it could literally be felt (Exodus 10:21-23).

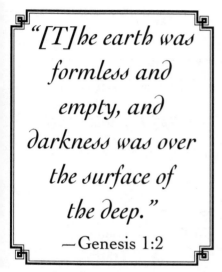

"[T]he earth was formless and empty, and darkness was over the surface of the deep."

—Genesis 1:2

Commentators propose that perhaps a sandstorm or a heavy fog may have precipitated the darkness, but regardless of the cause, one thing was certain: "all the Israelites had light in the places where they lived" (Exodus 10:23).

Even then, the contrast between God's chosen ones (people of light) and those who opposed Him (people of darkness) is very evident.

Turning over to the New Testament, we learn from three accounts of the crucifixion that there was darkness over the earth from noon until 3 p.m. on the day Jesus died (Matthew 27:45, Mark 15:33, Luke 23:44).

Poets and song writers throughout the years have made much of a symbolism involving God apparently turning away His face from His suffering Son.

"Well might the sun in darkness hide and shut his glories in," writes Isaac Watts in the familiar hymn *At the Cross*. "When Christ the mighty Maker died for man, the creature's sin."

Finally, darkness in scripture is used to delineate the eternal destination of those who spurn the mercy God offers. In Matthew 25, at the picture of the judgment scene, unprofitable servants are sentenced to a place of "outer darkness," where there will be weeping and gnashing of teeth (verses 30, 46).

What is the longest period of darkness you have ever experienced? What might your reaction have been as an Egyptian suffering through the ninth plague?

_____

_____

_____

DARKNESS AS IT RELATES TO FEAR AND DANGER

Most of us as children were probably afraid of the dark. Many adults never outgrow that fear.

What is it about darkness that causes such trepidation?

For one thing, some evil-doers consider darkness a cloak for their misdeeds.

Statistics prove that more bur-glaries take place between 6 p.m.

> *"More burglaries take place between 6 p.m. and 2 a.m. than any other time."*

and 2 a.m. than any other time. More murders are committed during hours of darkness than in hours of daylight.

While they certainly were not robbers or murderers, even the disciples in first century Damascus realized the secrecy afforded by nightfall. After Saul's conversion, when his life was endangered, the Christians waited until dark to help him escape. They knew they were less likely to be caught then as they lowered him over the city wall in a basket (Acts 9:19-25).

> *People with no exposure to light for an extended period of time have been known to lose their sanity.*

Darkness can be dangerous, not only because of those who would use it to hide their actions but also because without light it is impossible to see clearly.

A perfect example of this is an incident that happened to me several years ago when I was speaking at a ladies' retreat in Birmingham, Alabama. The retreat was held downtown at the old Tutwiler Hotel. The room where I was spending the night was lovely, but there was one slight problem. Its layout was totally different from the bedroom at home where my husband and I normally sleep. Upon awakening during the night, I got up to go to the restroom without turning on a lamp. Groggy, but confident I was in my own house, I merely headed in the direction of the bath that adjoins our master bedroom—and promptly crashed into a wall! (It hurt my nose *almost* as much as it hurt my pride.)

Without a doubt, darkness can cause both fear and danger. Long periods of it can result in depression. People with no exposure to light for an extended time have even been known to lose their sanity.

> How does your mood differ on a day that is bright and sunny compared to one that is dark and gloomy?
>
> Tired, lazy

GROWING ACCUSTOMED TO DARKNESS

What happens to your eyes when you first enter a theater after a performance has already begun? For the first few moments, you are unable to see anything at all because of the darkness. In time, however, your pupils adjust. You become accustomed to the lack of lighting and, eventually, can make your way to your seat.

The world in which we live today is plagued with the darkness of sin. Ephesians 6:12 says that, as Christians, our struggle is not against flesh and blood, but against "the powers of this dark world . . ." and "forces of evil."

If we are not careful, we can become accustomed to sin, just as our eyes become accustomed to darkness. In fact, in many areas, this may have already happened. A prime example is the entertainment industry in our country.

James Dobson, in his book *Stories of the Heart and Home*, discusses the change that has taken place in music in recent years. He notes that in 1953 the most popular song in the United States was a tune entitled "Oh,

> *Our struggle is not against flesh and blood, but against "the powers of this dark world . . ."*

My Papa" sung by Eddie Fisher. A portion of the lyrics were as follows:

> *Oh, my papa, to me he was so wonderful*
> *Oh, my papa, to me he was so good.*
> *No one could be so gentle and so loveable,*
> *Oh, my papa, he always understood.*

Once rock and roll came on the scene, music started to reflect the youthful rebellion that surfaced in the 1960's. It began almost humorously (an example is the number-one hit "Yakkety-Yak . . . Don't Talk Back") but began to turn bitter by the end of the decade. In "The End," a 1968 release by The Doors, Jim Morrison fantasized about killing his father. By 1984, Twisted Sister released "We're Not Gonna Take It," where a father is blasted out of a second-story apartment building window.

The theme of killing parents became a regular one in modern music, according to Dobson who quotes the following lyrics from Suicidal Tendencies' 1983 "I Saw Your Mommy":

> I saw your mommy and your mommy's dead.
> I watched her as she bled.
> Chewed-off toes on her chopped-off feet.
> I took a picture because I thought it was neat.

Next, a group known as Ice-T and Body Count came out with "Momma's Gonna Die Tonight," a song with lyrics too graphic to even quote.

In scarcely more than a generation, Dobson notes, the most popular music of our culture went from "Oh, My Papa" to the horrors of "Momma's Gonna Die Tonight."

And yet some of us barely noticed.

The same thing happened in the television and movie industries. Blatant

> *Blatant homosexuality and constant profanity crept in gradually . . . but then . . . became commonplace.*

homosexuality and constant profanity crept in gradually (remember our shock over Clark Gable's one curse word in "Gone with the Wind"?), but then daringly took hold and became commonplace. Nevertheless, ticket sales for movies continued to rise, and the number of television sets in American homes constantly increased.

How have television and movies changed in your lifetime?

homosexuality is a "norm"

language + nudity in commercials

OTHER EXAMPLES

The darkness that exists in our twenty-first century world can be evidenced in many additional areas.

Tucker Carlson, in the March 2003 issue of *Reader's Digest*, describes a class in Male Sexuality offered at the University of California, Berkeley, where students actually took pictures of their genitals, then shuffled the photographs in a box, and were challenged to match body parts to their classmates' faces. Other activities of the course, which Carlson dubs "Porn 101," included a lecture from an expert on sex toys and a field trip to a gay strip club where the course's instructor ended up having sex on stage!

The trend toward the obscene in the classroom is not limited to Berkeley. According to Carlson, San Francisco State University recently offered a course in Exploring Cybersexualities that gave students tips for finding pornography on the Internet. And in South Hadley, Massachusetts, a dean at Mount Holyoke College defended an erotic dance course taught by a former stripper who trained students for debuts in local clubs. "Stripping," he said, "seems to build self-esteem."

Another area that confirms the darkness of modern society is the frequency with which abortions take place. Some of our most visible celebrities—in Hollywood and Washington—have become animal rights activists and decry the abuse and mistreatment of pets, while the slaughter of millions of innocent babies goes virtually unnoticed.

Dr. Jean Staker Garton, an accomplished lecturer, teacher and author, was once a proponent of the pro-abortion movement as well as other feminist platforms. After thoroughly examining the evidence, however, Dr. Garton completely changed her mind on the issue and has become one of abortion's most vocal opponents.

In the book *Beyond Equal Rights*, she relates an incident that led to her reversal of opinions:

> *Some . . . decry the abuse and mistreatment of pets, while the slaughter of millions of innocent babies goes virtually unnoticed.*

All our children were in bed; the late television news was over, and I was putting the finishing touches to a presentation for medical students scheduled to be given the next day. As I reviewed some slides which might be used, there appeared on the screen a picture of an abortion victim, aged two and one-half months' gestation; her body had been dismembered by a curette, the long-handled knife used in a D&C abortion procedure.

Suddenly I heard, rather than saw, another person near me. At the sound of a sharp intake of breath, I turned to find that my youngest son, then a sleepy, rumpled three-year-old, had unexpectedly and silently entered the room. His small voice was filled with great sadness as he asked, "Who broke the baby?"

List other examples you can think of where, under the guise of "freedom," citizens have crossed the boundaries of what is right.

_____

_____

_____

THE DARKEST TIME EVER?

As we look around us at the problems in our twenty-first century world, it is easy to become discouraged and think that we are living in the most sinful society ever.

Is that the case?

Possibly, but before we become too disillusioned, it might be good to consider some dark periods in previous times.

Genesis 6:5 tells us that in the days of Noah "The Lord saw how great man's wickedness on the earth had become, and that every inclination of the thoughts of his heart was only evil all the time." Remember, in those days, only *eight* righteous people could be found in the entire world!

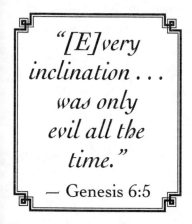

> *"[E]very inclination . . . was only evil all the time."*
> — Genesis 6:5

When it comes to bleak times, nothing in my mind can top a situation from 2 Kings 6 when the king of Syria had besieged Samaria. The famine had become so great that people were forced to eat dove droppings! Worse than that, though, two women actually agreed to an act of cannibalism involving their own offspring. How could a society sink any lower than one where a woman asks justice from the king because her friend refuses (as promised) to kill her son that they may eat him?

Then there are at least two periods recorded in Bible history where evil rulers, as a means of self-protection, ordered mass killings of children. Can you imagine being an expectant Hebrew mother and knowing that if you gave birth to a daughter, she would be permitted to live, but a son would automatically be thrown into the Nile River (Exodus 1:22)? Or can you imagine being the parent of an exuberant toddler who is whisked away from you simply because he has not yet celebrated his second birthday (Matthew 2:16)?

The very time period in which our Lord's church was established here on the earth could be said to be an epoch of moral darkness. Temple prostitution and human sacrifice were commonplace in cities such as Ephesus and Rome. And, of course, that was even *before* the persecution of Christians began.

Think of other examples from history when terrible atrocities were committed. List them below.

Hitler

SUMMARY

Our society today overflows with examples of the rule and power of Satan. From the taking of innocent lives—whether by terrorist attacks or by abortion—to sexual perversion and permissiveness, degradation abounds. If truth be told, however, such carnality is nothing new. The prince of darkness has long had control over men's hearts. In fact, ever since sin was first introduced to the world by Adam and Eve in the Garden of Eden, people have loved darkness rather than light (John 3:19).

This inclination is the very thing that brought God's Son down from heaven. "I have come into the world as a light," He said, "so that no one who believes in me should stay in darkness" (John 12:46).

Just as Jesus brought light to a darkened world, Christians are expected to be an illuminating presence to those around them.

We are a chosen people, Paul tells us in 1 Peter 2:9. A royal priesthood. A holy nation. A people belonging to God.

And our purpose? To "declare the praises of him who called you out of darkness into his wonderful light."

CHAPTER 2

The Source of Power: God Is Light

Today on my weekly run to the discount store, I placed in my shopping cart a package of light bulbs. They were greatly needed at home, especially considering the fact that in the last few days we've had two lamps and one overhead fixture go dark, and as luck would have it no replacements were anywhere in sight.

Funny thing, though, lying there in my buggy, those light bulbs hardly seemed to have the value their price tag demands. Why would I rush out to the store to buy them anyway? They gave off no light whatsoever.

Now I know what you're thinking: *Of course they didn't give off any light! Bulbs in and of themselves have no power to do that. In order to shine, they have to be connected to a source of electricity.* Exactly.

In a similar way, while we as Christians are admonished numerous times in scripture to be light in a darkened world, on our own we are as useless and unproductive as light bulbs still in their packaging. We glow when—and only when—we are connected to a power source. And the source of our power is God.

"GOD IS LIGHT"

1 John 1:5 tells us, "God is light; in him there is no darkness at all."

Later in the same letter, John gives another one-word description of the Father. There (1 John 4:8), he says, "God is love."

These short, precise statements are designed to convey the nature of the one who made us. God, as evidenced by His sacrificial sending of Jesus, is love personified. And just as He embodies all of the qualities that combine to create love, in Him are also incorporated the distinct characteristics of light.

Let's notice some of those characteristics.

(1) Splendor and glory. Anyone who has ever attended an NBA game understands the spectacular use of a spotlight. As the time for tip-off nears, anticipation mounts and a hush falls across the thousands of sports fans. A beam scans over the crowd while the announcer, with an appropriately booming voice, welcomes everyone to the arena. Then, one by one, starting players are announced and singled out by a distinguishing ray of light. Even if you are not a basketball aficionado, you cannot help but be captivated by the sheer drama of it.

Have you ever been in the spotlight? How did it make you feel?

_____

_____

_____

(I must admit I have even, on occasion, adapted this idea for the Bible school setting with some success. Imagine a darkened classroom and a flashlight focused on an embarrassed but secretly delighted student while a teacher proclaims: *And here he is, straight from Webster Elementary School. He stands four feet tall, made all A's last year, and loves cheese pizza. Give a warm welcome to . . . TYLER MADISON!* Compare *that* to sticking a star on an attendance chart!)

Somehow, light flooding all around you gives a sense of glory and importance.

One of my earliest film memories is watching *Your Cheating Heart* (the Hank Williams story) on NBC's long-running series, "Saturday Night at the Movies." For some odd reason, basically one scene from that show stands out in my mind. It is at the end of the film when the young country music star has died on his way to a performance. As I recall, the final image is of a darkened stage and a spotlight beaming down on an empty microphone. The brilliant light shines, representing, I suppose, a splendor and glory—albeit an earthly one—that has been extinguished.

In scripture, there are numerous instances where the divine nature of the Godhead is symbolized by brightness.

In the Old Testament, when Moses came down from Mt. Sinai with tablets of stone containing the Ten Commandments tucked under his arms, the Bible says his face was "radiant" or "shone," to such an extent that he finally had to wear a veil! The Israelites immediately understood that the glow was a result of his having been in the presence of the Father (Exodus 34:29-35).

Remember the bright light that beamed down on Saul on the road to Damascus? (Acts 9:1-19) That was God! It caused Saul to fall to the

ground in awe; in fact, coming in contact with that God of light changed his
life forever.

Then, consider the incident that
took place on the Mount of Transfigu-
ration (Luke 9:28-35). What occurred
there was not, as we often suppose, the
Son of God taking on a different nature or appearance. It was, rather, His
stripping away a temporary facade to

> *Remember the bright light that beamed down on Saul on the road to Damascus? That was God!*

reveal Himself as He truly is ("dazzling," according to the New American
Standard Version).

Revelation tells us that in heaven we will not need a lamp or even the
sun anymore because God will be there (Revelation 22:5). (Just think,
no more electric bills! Will *that* not be heavenly?) His presence is the
ultimate in majesty and splendor. No wonder the saved, surrounding His
throne, will be content for all eternity, just basking in the wonder of it!

I love the story told of a little girl walking outside with her father one
evening. Looking up at the glorious sky above her, she said, "Just think,
Daddy, how wonderful heaven must be if it's like this wrong side out!"

(2) *Purity and holiness.* In his commentary on 1 John, Burton Coffman
says that light is a symbol of all that is "lovely, beautiful, holy, good, de-
sirable, righteous . . . " Just as the statement "God is light" speaks of the
splendor of our Maker, it also addresses His sinlessness.

What happens when you go to the hospital to see a newborn these
days? Things have changed significantly in the medical field in recent
times, and now most everyone—even young siblings—are permitted immediate and direct contact with the infant. In most cases, however, I have
found that new parents have one stipulation before they let you hold their
baby (and rightly so): *"Please wash your hands."* That is pretty much basic
procedure, and I am not offended at all when asked to do so. Why? Because babies are pure and we are not! Care must be taken so as not to
contaminate them with germs from the outside world.

In a similar way, God is pure. In Isaiah's vision (Isaiah 6:3), the ser-
aph cry, "Holy, holy, holy is the Lord of hosts" (KJV). Repetition of the

Why is washing of hands so important? What instances can you think of where it is required? Why?

before eating

after playing outside

word "holy" implies absolute holiness or holiness to a superlative degree. Sin is contrary to God's nature; He has never been (nor will ever be) contaminated with anything unclean.

Not long after my husband's father passed away, his mother came to our home for an extended visit. I was thrilled to have her, but naturally a little self-conscious as she observed me in my normal daily routines. Even though I had been her daughter-in-

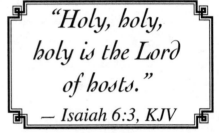

"Holy, holy, holy is the Lord of hosts."
— Isaiah 6:3, KJV

law a long time, she had rarely stayed with us, and I was still eager for her approval.

Getting ready to put in a load of clothes one morning, I casually mentioned that I was laundering whites and asked if she had anything that needed washing. She gave me a white half-slip. You can imagine my mortification later that day when I went to remove the clothes and realized that her slip was no longer white but pink. Without realizing it, I had left the washer setting on hot water, and a white basketball jersey in the load just happened to have a tiny red trim around the sleeves. In the hot water, the red had faded, causing a distinct discoloration to all the clothing in the machine (not to mention a distinct embarrassment to one horrified daughter-in-law!).

There is not a hint, not even a tiny trace of impurity in our God. When we consider this holiness and then look at ourselves in comparison, the contrast is overwhelming. Funny lady Erma Bombeck had a famous prayer she penned: "Lord, make me skinny; and if You can't do that, sur-

those around us, and doing that, we come out all right. But when we compare ourselves with the purity and holiness—the *perfection*—of the Father, then we come up terribly short.

(3) *Self-revealing.* In Genesis 29, we read that Laban gave Leah, his elder weak-eyed daughter, to Jacob instead of Rachel, the one who had been promised (and for whom Jacob had worked seven long years!). In the evening, when the marriage took place, Jacob was unaware of Laban's deception. But the light of morning (Genesis 29:25) revealed his bride's true identity.

Light has a way of doing that—showing things as they really are. Several years ago I purchased a skirt and sweater from separate racks in a clothing store, assuming them to be the same color. They certainly appeared that way under the florescent bulbs in the dressing room! But when I got the outfit home (or rather wore it in public the first time), I found, to my chagrin, it didn't match at all. The true light of day proved the colors to be two completely different shades.

When I was in high school, the mother of one of my friends decided to give her daughter a surprise party for her fifteenth birthday. As part of the surprise, she invited my friend's pen pal (a boy who lived in another part of the state). He and my friend had never met, but they had been exchanging letters for quite some time and seemed to be very compatible. So, my friend's mother thought it would be fun to include him in the festivities. Upon his arrival, she even convinced him (how, I am not quite sure!) to get inside a large refrigerator box she had decorated appropriately. When my friend appeared, we all yelled, "Surprise!" and then immediately directed her attention to the over-sized present. "Open it," we admonished her.

Talk about disaster. I will never forget the look on my friend's face as she ripped away the wrapping and out popped this total stranger. "Who

> Think of a time when you were deceived by a lack of complete honesty. Are we ever guilty of only partial revelation to others? Why?
>
> _____
>
> _____
>
> _____

are *you*?" she asked, and it was basically downhill from there. It turned out to be quite a nightmare because this young man was a little different (Who am I kidding? He was a *lot* different) than he had led my friend to believe. He had revealed only certain things he wanted her to know (made some of them up, I think!) and had *not* revealed other things.

God is not that way. He has shown us Himself in His Word, His true nature. There will be no surprises for us on Judgment Day. He is as He says He is.

Have you ever thought that God did not have to tell us about heaven and hell? He could have just told us what we were to do and left it at that, and then either rewarded or punished us ac-

> *There will be no surprises . . . on Judgment Day. God is as He says He is.*

cordingly. But that is not the route He chose. Instead, He has revealed Himself to us, and I for one am thankful that we do not have to sit back in fear and dread and wonder what He is like.

As someone has said, "You *can* know God. He is an open book."

No Power On Our Own

Certainly, the source of our power is God. Any illumination that exudes from us comes directly from Him and not through anything we produce on our own. "For thou dost light my lamp" (NAS), we are told in Psalm 18:28.

"Power," David reaffirmed in Psalm 62:11, "belongs to God" (NAS).

Throughout scripture, we see numerous instances where people were powerless.

Joshua 8 records the story of the second attack on the city of Ai. The first one, you remember, had been disastrous—the Israelites' lone defeat in their conquest of Canaan (a result of Achan's disobedience regarding the spoils from Jericho). The second time around, though, things were different. Instead of strolling in haughtily as before, this time the children of Israel—listening to their God—had a plan. Joshua instructed a group of 30,000 soldiers to lie in ambush behind the city. Meanwhile, he and a second battalion entered Ai and attacked. When the inhabitants of Ai responded, Joshua's group, feigning defeat, fled from the city. As men of Ai followed, the soldiers in ambush emerged, captured the city, and set fire to it. Verse 20 says, "And when the men of Ai looked behind them, they saw, and behold, the smoke of the city ascended up to heaven, and they had no power to flee this way or that. . . "

> *"[T]he smoke of the city ascended up to heaven, and they had no power to flee. . ."*
>
> — *Joshua 8:20; KJV*

Caught in a crossfire, these people were helpless. They recognized that there was nothing they could do that would alter their situation.

Many times, unfortunately, we are like the people of Ai. Because of a victory experienced in the past—one we are convinced is of our doing—we head out, filled with false confidence, ready to take on the world. Suddenly, however, we find ourselves surrounded on every side with nowhere to turn. Where is our power then?

Another example is found in Numbers 22. In this highly entertaining incident, we find that the cinema's Dr. Dolittle has nothing on God's prophet. Balaam also "talked to the animals," and they—at least one, a donkey—talked to him!

At this particular time, Balak, the king of Moab, was feeling nervous, having heard all kinds of rumors about the advancing army of Israelites. Looking for assistance anywhere he could find it, he sent a convoy to Balaam, trying to persuade him to come and place a curse on God's people. Although Balaam knew up front he could not do that, he was obviously tempted. Instead of immediately negating the proposition, he hesitated, inviting the messengers to spend the night (along with a second group that came later), and ended up eventually giving in. (What a lesson for us!) On the journey—by means of a very uncooperative donkey—God expressed His displeasure with Balaam's decision. He did, however, permit Balaam to continue, instructing him to speak only the words he would be given. The prophet apparently yielded to God; for when he finally arrived in Moab, he told the king, "Have I any power at all . . . ?"

Has there ever been an occasion when you were completely powerless? How did that make you feel?

_____

_____

_____

_____

A third example comes from 2 Chronicles 20. Near the end of Jehoshaphat's reign, a powerful group—consisting of the children of Moab, the children of Ammon and some Edomites—came to fight against Judah. Described as a "great multitude" (KJV), the armies were quite intimidating. Jehoshaphat, though admittedly alarmed, "resolved to inquire of the Lord" (2 Chronicles 20:3) and proclaimed a fast. The Bible tells us that people from every town came together "to seek help from the Lord" (2 Chronicles 20:4). What a beautiful example of both capable leadership and a unified response!

Speaking before the assembly at the temple, the king assessed Judah's capabilities ("we have no power to face this vast army," 2 Chronicles 20:12) and acknowledged dependence upon another source ("Power and might are in your hand," 2 Chronicles 12:6).

God, apparently touched by their humility, replied through a man named Jahaziel, assuring them that victory would be theirs, and they would not even have to be involved in it. "For the battle is not yours, but God's," he said (2 Chronicles 20:15). "You will not have to fight. . . .Take up your positions; stand firm and see the deliverance the Lord will give you" (2 Chronicles 20:17). Sure enough, the Lord intervened, and the armies ended up destroying one another.

> *"Power and might are in your hand."*
> — *2 Chronicles 20:6*

Like the characters in these stories, we should realize this: (1) on our own, we are lost and helpless with nowhere to turn; (2) we need to yield our will to the Father; and (3) if we do that, then He will provide the power we need in our lives.

What God's Light Gives Us

This God of ours who is light has made it possible for us to be connected to numerous things. These include the Gospel, Salvation, Knowledge, and Life:

(1) The Gospel: In 2 Corinthians 4:4, Paul says that "the god of this world" (KJV) (Satan) keeps unbelievers from seeing "the light of the gospel." But those of us who believe have access to this enlightening gospel, which, according to Philippians 1:7, makes us partakers of God's grace.

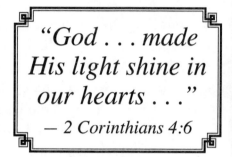

> "*God . . . made His light shine in our hearts . . .*"
> *— 2 Corinthians 4:6*

(2) Salvation: "The Lord is my light and my salvation," David wrote in Psalm 27:1. In Acts 13, when Paul and Barnabas were speaking to the Jews in Antioch, Paul said that the Lord had set him as a light to the Gentiles "that you may bring salvation to the ends of the earth" (Acts 13:47).

(3) Knowledge: 2 Corinthians 4:6 says, "For God, who said, 'Let light shine out of darkness,' made his light shine in our hearts to give us the light of the knowledge of the glory of God. . . . "

(4) Life: "For you have delivered my soul from death," the Psalmist wrote in Psalms 56:13, "and my feet from stumbling, that I may walk before God in the light of life." In Matthew 4, when Jesus had left Nazareth to begin His ministry in Capernaum, the writer tells us that He fulfilled the prophecy of Isaiah: "the people living in darkness have seen a great light; on those living in the land of the shadow of death a light has dawned" (Matthew 4:16).

What things are made possible by physical light? Now list some things that are a result of spiritual light.

_____

_____

_____

_____

SUMMARY

Just as light bulbs must be connected to a power source before they can shine, we as Christians must be connected to God who, throughout Scripture, is associated with the idea of light.

In fact, the first recorded words spoken by God in the Bible are, "Let there be light" (Genesis 1:3). 1 John 1:5 tells us, "God is light, in him is no darkness at all."

Light has many distinctive qualities. It is a symbol of splendor and glory, it represents purity and holiness, and it is also self-revealing. Each of these characteristics also describes the nature of God.

As human beings, we are helpless and hopeless on our own. We need to connect ourselves to the Father and yield our will to His.

Only through Him and the good news of His Gospel can we tap into salvation, knowledge, and life.

CHAPTER 3

The Illumination: God's Word Is Light

In the days following the horrific events of September 11, like most Americans, I stayed glued to my television set and read almost anything I could get my hands on that had to do with the tragedy.

One of the most interesting items I came across was an article in the September 14 issue of *USA Today*. Authored by a reporter named Andrea Stone, the piece detailed conditions at the Pentagon, which had been struck earlier that week by hijacked American Airlines Flight 77. Army Staff Sergeant Mark Williams, one of the first recovery personnel to enter the military headquarters, battled 120-degree heat and found sights so gruesome, "I wanted to cry from the minute I walked in."

"It was the worst thing you can imagine," he was quoted as saying.

Despite his difficult task—removing charred corpses of military workers from their desks and airline passengers, still strapped in, from their seats—Williams was moved by something unexpected.

> *[S]earchers who had gotten a close look said it was a Bible. It was not burned.*

"[A]s he looked up into the black chasm torn into the symbol of the mightiest military in the world," Stone wrote, "Williams saw a sign of hope. On a second floor, right next to where the jet sheared off a section of the building, was an undisturbed stool. And on it was a thick, open book. Fellow searchers who had gotten a close look said it was a Bible. It was not burned. Nor was anything around it or on the two floors above it."

I found the incident intriguing (not to mention the fact that it was actually reported in a national newspaper!), but I was not prepared for what happened next. A few days later, my husband brought home a special edition copy of a news magazine that reviewed the recent acts of terrorism. As we poured over page after page of photographs, one particular shot of the Pentagon caught our eye. Though there was no mention of it whatsoever

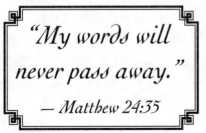

> *"My words will never pass away."*
> — Matthew 24:35

on that page or anywhere else in the magazine, a stool with an open, untouched book was very visible among the debris!

How fitting, we agreed, that a written treatise containing God's Word withstand such an attack. After all, did Jesus not say, "Heaven and earth will pass away, but my words will never pass away" (Matthew 24:35)?

A LAMP TO MY FEET

As we saw in the previous chapter, God is light and the source of all power. Because of Him, we are no longer confined to a world of darkness. Psalm 36:9 says, "[I]n your light, we see light."

Besides God Himself, however, there is something else that illuminates our way.

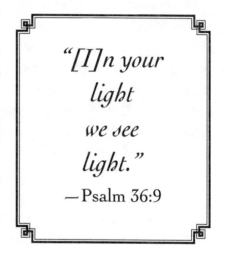

"[I]n your light we see light."

—Psalm 36:9

"Your word," the Psalmist penned in Psalm 119:105, "is a lamp to my feet and a light for my path."

When my husband and I worked with the young people in our local congregation, we once planned an outing to a cornfield maze in a nearby state. Thanks to some ingenious farmers, such mazes had become all the rage in the Southeast. This particular one had been cut into the shape of the continental U.S. It was fascinating—and fun—to try to find our way through borders of the 48 states. I mention that it was fun, however, only because our efforts were expended on a sunny Saturday morning. Had we attempted to navigate the course, say, on a dark, moonless evening, we would not have been nearly as successful—or have enjoyed it nearly as much!

In darkness, it is difficult to see. Light becomes a necessity to help one find the way. This is the purpose that God's Word serves in our lives. Not only does it reveal Him to us, it enlightens our path so that we can find the true and safe route. Without it, we would surely stumble and fall or lose our way.

In what ways does God's Word give us direction? Think of other analogies for what God's Word represents to us, and list them below.

_____

_____

_____

_____

THE MOST AMAZING CHAPTER IN THE BIBLE

Psalm 119:105, alluded to earlier, is one of the most famous verses in all of Scripture. It has even been put to music so that we can sing it. While it may be better known than its surrounding context, however, the passage itself is far from unique. In the chapter where it is found—the longest, by the way, in all the Bible—175 other verses all discuss the very same topic! Every single thought in this lengthy section deals with some facet of God's Word. And what is so fascinating about it is the manner in which it is written.

An old song from the 1960's began:

"**A**, you're adorable,

B, you're so beautiful,

C, you're a cutie full of charms;

D, you're delightful and,

E, you're exciting, and

F, you're a feather in my arms. . . "

Basically the same style of that refrain is employed in this psalm. All letters of the Hebrew alphabet—there are 22 of them—appear in order. The chapter has 22 paragraphs, and each paragraph starts with a letter of the alphabet. Not only that, but each paragraph has eight lines, and each line also starts with that same letter! Unfortunately, we lose the full effect because when it is translated into English, the letters are not all the same. But it is pretty incredible to read in the original language (or so I have been told).

I cannot help but wonder if the writer did not purposefully choose this remarkable style of writing to showcase what he believed to be a most remarkable topic. God's Word, he affirms through the intricacies of the poem, is everything to us—everything, as we who speak English might say, from A to Z.

Scholars have noted that in each of the 176 verses in this phenomenal chapter, God is either referred to or addressed. And every verse—with the exception of 122— contains the word "law" or else a synonym for it (these include: *word, saying, commandment, statute, ordinance, precept, testimony, way, path, truth*).

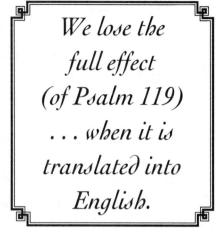

We lose the full effect (of Psalm 119) . . . when it is translated into English.

Matthew Henry, in recounting the life of his father Philip Henry, remembered being advised to take one verse of Psalm 119 every day and meditate on it. By doing so, one could go through the entire passage twice in a year. "That," the elderly Henry said, "will bring you to be in love with all the rest of the Scriptures."

Charles Spurgeon, in his book *Psalms*, tells an interesting anecdote relating to Psalm 119. According to him, a man named George Wishart would have died by hanging had he not taken advantage of a custom that allowed a condemned man to select a psalm to be sung. Wishart chose the lengthy Psalm 119, and before all of it had been sung, he received a pardon that spared his life!

Using the letters of the alphabet, think of as many adjectives as you can to describe what God's Word means to you.

_____

_____

_____

_____

_____

_____

AMAZING VERSES

Let's notice just a few verses from this extraordinary chapter.

Verse 16 says, "I delight in your decrees; I will not neglect your word." According to commentator Adam Clarke, the first part of this statement suggests, "I will skip about and jump for joy!"

Have you ever been so excited about something that you literally jumped up and down? I remember an incident from high school. My mother bought two large gold frames from a quaint little shop in a nearby town to display some oil portraits of my sister and me. With her purchase, she became eligible to enter an upcoming drawing where the grand prize would be a large, beautiful ornate mirror (that just happened to match the frames perfectly). One afternoon several weeks later, she received a phone call, and I do not think I will ever forget her reaction. When the store manager informed her that she had won the drawing, she was ecstatic. She jumped up and down, yelled and screamed, and gave the young man who was visiting me at the time every reason to think she had completely lost her mind!

> Think of an instance where you literally jumped up and down for joy. What was the cause of your jubilation? Now think of a spiritual memory of equal exuberance.
>
> _____
>
> _____
>
> _____

A few years ago, our family attended a basketball game where a player on our school's team hit a long three-point shot right at the buzzer to give us our first lead in the entire game and a victory to boot. As we all spilled down onto the court from the bleachers, the player's parents—much to his dismay—could not contain their jubilation. His father literally picked up his mother and swung her around in a circle, much as one would do with a child!

Do we delight in God's Word? Does it fill us with joy? Are we overcome with emotion because of it? According to Psalm 119:16, we should be.

A second verse from the chapter, verse 31, states, "I hold fast to your statutes, O Lord; do not let me be put to shame." The New King James Version says, "I cling to your testimonies," while the King James is translated, "I have stuck unto thy testimonies." The Hebrew word in the first part of the phrase literally means *glued to.* Dr. James Dobson, in one of his books, tells about a young mother who had been cooped up for days with a lively toddler. In a desperate attempt to get out of the house, she decided she would take him to a movie. He had never been to one before, but she was confident it would entertain him and thus give her a little peace and rest. Upon arrival at the theater, however, they discovered a minor problem: he did not weigh enough to hold one of the seats down! So he was forced to sit—squirming, of course—in her lap. During the next two hours, thanks to his wiggles, they managed to spill a king-size soda and a large box of buttery popcorn. The syrupy combination oozed all over the child and ran into the mother's lap and down her legs. With the movie nearing its conclusion, however, instead of leaving immediately, she decided to wait and clean up later. What she did not realize was that, as they sat there, she and her son were being gradually cemented together! According to Dobson, when the film ended, they stood up and the mother's wraparound skirt came unwrapped. It stuck to the bottom of the little boy as he scampered up the aisle away from her! She watched in horror, clutching her slip (and thanking the good Lord she had taken the time to put one on!). Now, *that's* the idea of holding fast!

A similar idea is stated over in the New Testament where we are told by the Hebrew writer, "Let us hold unswervingly to the hope we profess, for he who promised is faithful" (Hebrews 10:23).

> *"Let us hold unswervingly to the hope we profess . . ."*
> *— Hebrews 10:23*

A third verse from Psalm 119, verse 59 says, "I thought on my ways, and turned my feet unto thy testimonies" (KJV). The words "thought on my ways" carry with them the idea of considering one's conduct from all sides. (Remember, as parents, sending a disobedient child to his or her room with the instructions to "think about what you have done"?) In Hebrew, this phrase is a metaphor from a type of embroidery where the figure must appear the same on one side as it does on the other. (How hard would *that* be to accomplish?) The fabric has to be turned and checked every time the needle is set in. In this same manner, the psalmist seems to say, *we need to diligently examine what we do and make sure our footsteps are in accordance to God's Word.*

One final verse to consider from this chapter is verse 131. It states, "I open my mouth and pant, longing for your commands," or as the ASV translates, "I opened wide my mouth." In this statement, the psalmist appears to use a mixed metaphor. The panting indicates an exhausted animal in need of fresh air or water; the "open mouth," however, implies the idea of tiny birds, ready and waiting to receive food from the mother bird. Both of these images from the animal kingdom convey the attitude we need to have to God's Word.

Webster defines pant as "to long eagerly; yearn." This same word is used in Psalm 42:1 for a thirsty animal seeking out refreshment. We read, "As the deer pants for the water brooks, so pants my soul for You, O God" (NAS). In the Sermon on the Mount, Jesus praised those "who hunger and thirst for righteousness" and said that their need would be satisfied (Matthew 5:6). Job 5:5 speaks of those who would pant after or desire things of a worldly nature, such as the wealth of a fool. Rather than eagerly longing for material objects, we should desire "the sincere milk of the word" (1 Peter 2:2, KJV).

The idea of having an open mouth suggests that we need to be ready and eager to accept God's Word and realize that through it we receive our nourishment. "I am the Lord your God . . ." we are told in Psalm 81:10. "Open wide your mouth and I will fill it."

What is the longest you have ever gone without eating? What is the longest you have ever gone without partaking of God's Word?

_____

_____

_____

_____

ENLIGHTENED EYES

Another passage that presents to us the important role of God's Word in our lives is Psalm 19. Verses 7-10 of that chapter, very familiar to most, read:

> The law of the Lord is perfect, reviving the soul.
>
> The statutes of the Lord are trustworthy, making wise the simple.
>
> The precepts of the Lord are right, giving joy to the heart.
>
> The commands of the Lord are radiant, giving light to the eyes.
>
> The fear of the Lord is pure, enduring forever.
>
> The ordinances of the Lord are sure and altogether righteous.
>
> They are more precious than gold, than much pure gold;
>
> they are sweeter than honey, than honey from the comb.

In this passage, the worth of God's Word is compared to an abundance of fine gold, and the satisfaction it gives is compared to honey.

As all students of the Bible know, honey was a favorite Jewish food and had numerous uses. In addition to being included in medicinal remedies, it was also employed as a sweetener, and served as a primary ingredient in cakes and pastries (Ezekiel 16:13). The manna God sent the children of Israel in the wilderness is said to have had the taste of "wafers made with honey" (Exodus 16:31). Apparently, bees were plentiful in Palestine, and though the phrase cannot be taken literally, the description of Canaan as a land "flowing with milk and honey" (Exodus 3:8) suggests metaphorically that Palestine was a land of bounty.

Honey was a favorite Jewish food. Still today, it is rather remarkable. What are some of its benefits? How can it be compared to the Bible?

_____

_____

_____

_____

The second phrase in Psalm 19:8 is particularly arresting. The King James Version says, "[T]he commandment of the Lord is pure, enlightening the eyes." To clarify the expression, "enlightening the eyes," many Bible scholars refer back to an incident recorded in 1 Samuel 14.

Jonathan, the son of King Saul, had left his father's camp for the Philistines' garrison to do battle. Being away, he was unaware of a commandment Saul had given, stating that no one should eat anything until sundown (1 Samuel 14:24). Thus, when Jonathan came upon some honey on the ground in the forest, he did not hesitate, but reached out the end of the staff that was in his hand and dipped it in the honeycomb. "He raised his hand to his mouth," the Bible tells us, "and his eyes brightened." In other words, he was physically revived or refreshed. Fatigue and hunger affect the body's ability to function normally (even possibly dimming one's vision, some think). Taking in food, however, has an immediate impact, restoring metabolism. Jonathan goes on to say that had Saul's soldiers eaten that day—as he had—they most likely would have been physically stronger and able to destroy even more Philistines than they did!

God's Word, the Psalmist seems to tell us, refreshes the heart of man, just as honey refreshes the body. It is a "pick-me-up"; it gives strength. Certainly, our victories would be greater if we would dip into God's Word more often.

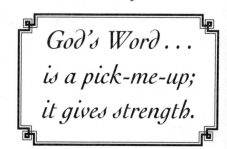

God's Word . . . is a pick-me-up; it gives strength.

"THE BEST THERE IS IN THE WORLD"

It has been written that prisoners who participated in the "Bataan Death March" of World War II valued the Bibles that were given to them. The reason they were thrilled to get them, though, might not be what you would first think. Instead of cherishing them because they provided words of comfort and courage for a difficult time, they were excited because the thin paper on which they were printed could be easily used for rolling cigarettes!

In an article entitled "Perspective" in *Herald of Holiness* (June 1992), W.E. McCumber wrote, "They valued smoke in their lungs more than truth in their hearts."

By contrast, those of us who are Christians know the true value of scriptures. As someone has said, they are "the traveler's map, the pilot's compass, the soldier's sword."

Woodrow Wilson once stated, "A man has deprived himself of the best there is in the world who has deprived himself of a knowledge of the Bible."

> How many Bibles do you own personally? Do you ever take this great treasure for granted?
>
> _____
>
> _____

WINNING THE BATTLE

A little boy once misunderstood the words of a popular church hymn. Instead of singing, "Revive us again," he sang, "Re-Bible us again." Maybe that is not such a bad version after all. We need to go back to God's Word. It is the only thing that can teach us how to live in such a way that we will be a shining light to those around us.

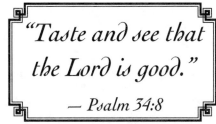

I once heard about a converted Indian who described the battle between good and evil that goes on within a Christian. He said, "It's like I have two dogs living inside me—a good dog and a bad dog. They are always fighting. The mean dog wants me to do bad things, and the good dog wants me to do good things. Do you know which dog wins? *The one I feed the most!*"

We need to feed our good dogs more! We need to feed—and not only feed but *feast*—on the Word of God.

As Psalm 34:8 says, "Taste and see that the Lord is good."

SUMMARY

Knowing well the darkness in which we live, our God of light has given us something to illuminate our pathway. That something is His Word.

Psalm 119, the longest chapter in the Bible, extols the virtues of scripture and teaches us the attitude we should have toward it. We should delight in it, long for it, cling to it, and make our life's decisions based upon it.

CHAPTER 4

The Reflection: God's People Are Light

Dr. Paul Brand, well-known for two decades of pioneering research on the disease of leprosy in India, writes of an interesting experience in the opening pages of *In His Image*, a book he co-authored with Philip Yancey.

One day while working with a group of interns and medical students at the Christian Medical College Hospital in Vellore, Dr. Brand could not help but notice that the bedside manner of one of his young trainees was eerily familiar. An upturned eyebrow, tilted head, and sympathetic smile all bore an uncanny resemblance, he realized, to Professor Robin Pilcher, who had been his chief surgeon back in London years earlier! "It seemed," he says, "as if the intern had studied Professor Pilcher's face for an acting audition and was now drawing from his repertoire to impress me."

How in the world, he wondered, could expressions of professional concern for a patient be so similar, when he knew for a certainty that the student had never been to England and also that Pilcher had never visited India?

Voicing his observations to the group around him, the doctor noticed several of the students smiling. "We don't know any Professor Pilcher," one of them said. "But Dr. Brand, that was *your* expression (the intern) was wearing."

> *He did not realize how many ... mannerisms he himself had imitated and had, unknowingly, passed on.*

Brand goes on to write that until that day he did not realize how many of Pilcher's mannerisms he himself had imitated and had, unknowingly, passed on to his protégés.

[I] thought back to my days under Pilcher. I had thought I was learning from him techniques of surgery and diagnostic procedures. But he had also imprinted his instincts, his expression, his very smile so that they, too, would be passed down from generation to generation ...

[I], Pilcher's student, had become a link in the chain, a carrier of his wisdom to students some nine thousand miles away. The Indian doctor, young and brown-skinned, speaking in Tamil, shared few obvious resemblances with either Pilcher or me. Yet somehow he had conveyed the likeness of my old chief so accurately that it had transported me back to university days with a start.

This story illustrates an important Biblical principle. As "sons of the light" (1 Thessalonians 5:5), Christians are to be a reflection of the Father, manifesting His qualities before the world.

Just as Brand—unknowingly—modeled for others the actions of his mentor, we need to display the traits of the Great Physician in our lives. "Be imitators of God," Paul wrote in Ephesians 5:1.

Think of someone in your past who you have admired and tried to imitate. How did you go about trying to be like that person?

_____

_____

_____

_____

"CANNOT BE HID"

Just what does it mean if the light of the Father is in us? According to Matthew 5:14, that light is going to be very visible to all around. He uses an illustration that is easily understood: "A city that is set on a hill cannot be hid."

When I think of something that cannot be hidden, I think of the story of baby Moses over in the book of Exodus. He was, you remember, born in the time of that terrible edict in Egypt when all baby boys were to be killed to prevent the growth of the Israelite nation. What did Jochebed, Moses' mother, do when he was born? She could not kill her baby—what mother could?—so she hid him as long as possible. But when he got to be three months old, he could not be hidden any longer. He was getting bigger, I imagine. He was sleeping less, and probably crying louder! So that is when she made a basket of bulrushes and put him in the Nile River where he was eventually found by the daughter of Pharaoh.

Imagine that you were Jochebed. How hard would it be to hide an infant from authorities for three months? What would that entail?

_____

_____

_____

Some things are hard to hide. But if I am a Christian, if I have given my life to the Lord, then I am not going to try to keep it a secret. I could not—even if I wanted to! It is like a young girl becoming engaged or a young married couple finding out that they are going to be parents—you want everyone to know.

In John 3, we read about a man named Nicodemus coming to see Jesus. Nicodemus was a Pharisee, a member of the Sanhedrin court and, more than likely, part of a distinguished Jewish family. William Barclay's commentary tells us that in 63 B.C. when the Jews and the Romans were at war, a man named Nicodemus was sent by the Jewish leaders as an ambassador to the Roman emperor, Pompey. This could very easily have been an ancestor of the man who visited Jesus.

Because John's gospel tells us that Nicodemus came to the Lord "at night," many suppose it was something he wanted to hide or to keep secret. An alternative view, proposed by Barclay, springs from the rabbis' belief that the most suitable time to ponder the law was at nighttime when a man was undisturbed. Since Jesus was surrounded throughout the daylight hours with crowds clamoring for His attention, Nicodemus could have chosen an evening encounter because he longed for a private conversation, without interruption.

Regardless of any initial reservations he may or may not have had, Nicodemus was intrigued enough by Jesus' reputation to seek Him out, and what followed was a stimulating discussion of rebirth. (Our Savior blew Nicodemus' mind by purporting an act he considered a physical impossibility. "How can a man be born when he is old?" he asked. "Surely he cannot enter a second time into his mother's womb!")

Nicodemus may have left that meeting confused; yet, by the next time he is mentioned in scripture, he seems to have grown a bit bolder where Jesus is concerned. In John 7, when officers return to the Pharisees without bringing back Jesus, as they had been instructed to do, the Jewish leaders are indignant. Nicodemus speaks up with a statement reminiscent of our American "innocent until proven guilty" philosophy. "Does our law condemn a man," he asks, "without first hearing him to find out what he is doing?"

> *By the time a third mention of Nicodemus is made in the New Testament, there seems to be nothing at all hidden about his feelings.*

By the time a third mention of Nicodemus is made in the New Testament, there seems to be nothing at all hidden about his feelings for—and commitment to—Jesus. After the crucifixion, Joseph of Arimathea (described as a "rich" and "prominent" man, but also a secret follower) went to Pilate, requested the body that had been taken down from the cross, and proceeded to bury it in a rock-hewn tomb where no one had ever been lain before. He was joined by Nicodemus, who brought one hundred pounds of myrrh and aloes, and the two of them wrapped the Lord's body in linen strips, along with the spices, in keeping with the custom of the Jews.

The death of Jesus, according to Barclay, seems to have done for Joseph and Nicodemus what even His life could not do. "The cowardice, the hesitation, the prudent concealment were gone. Those who had been afraid when Jesus was alive declared for Him in a way that everyone could see as soon as He was dead."

"CHILDREN OF LIGHT"

Ephesians 5:8 tells us, "For you were once darkness, but now you are light in the Lord. Live as children of light."

Just what does it mean to live as children of light?

(1) To live as children of light means a disconnection with the past. A little further down in Ephesians 5, Paul admonishes, "Have nothing to do with the fruitless deeds of darkness" (verse 11).

1 Peter 2:9 says we have been called "out of darkness," implying it is something connected with our old life, something to be left behind.

Paul's life of light certainly meant a disconnection with his past. Following his conversion in Acts 9, when he literally "saw the light" (a phrase that has come to be symbolic with change), he left behind everything he had previously been. As far as his identity, he was changed from Saul into Paul. As far as his ambition, he was changed from a persecutor of the church into a promoter. He went from putting Christians into prison to being an imprisoned Christian himself. In fact, it was from a prison in Rome that he penned these famous words, "Forgetting what is behind and straining toward what is ahead, I press on toward the goal to win the prize for which God has called me. . . " (Philippians 3:13,14).

> *Paul's life of light certainly meant a disconnection with his past.*

(2) To live as children of light means a determination for goodness. Matthew 5:16 says, "Let your light so shine before men, that they may see your good works. . . " (KVJ).

Goodness is not a quality we naturally possess; in fact, Psalm 14:3 tells us, "there is no one who does good, not even one." Jesus said, in Mark 10:18, "No one is good—except God alone." Because of what God has done for us, however, and because of the salvation He has made possible, goodness becomes something for which we strive. Ephesians 2:10 says, "For we are God's workmanship, created *in Christ Jesus* (or, literally, *on account of what He has done*) to do good works. . . " (emphasis mine).

F.C. Cook in his commentary on this verse makes what I think is a great point. He says everything has a purpose—lungs are made to breathe, eyes are made to see, etc. Even so, Christians are made for good works. But—and this is the part we need to remember—no merit is given to the lungs for breathing or the eyes for seeing. We do not gush and rave and say, "Oh, lungs, you are so wonderful! Look at how you inhale and exhale!" No, we do not make a big deal about it because *that is what lungs are supposed to do.* In a similar way, Christians are supposed to do good works. It should be as automatic to us as breathing in and out. We should do it almost without thinking.

Now, granted, there are those who take this "good works" idea to the extreme, claiming that by works we earn our salvation. Nothing could be further from the truth. Those who spout that philosophy remind me of the prodigal son in Luke 15, determining to ask his father for a job as a hired servant and work his way back into the family mansion. (His father, of course, would not hear of it. He wanted him back as a son!) God's acceptance of us has nothing to do with works, and everything to do with grace (Paul emphasized this very thing two verses earlier in Ephesians 2:8).

> The prodigal son felt he needed to work to earn a position in his father's family. Do we ever make that same mistake in our thinking? What part do works play in the life of a Christian?
>
> _____
>
> _____
>
> _____

We are not saved by works. We are saved *for* works, in order that we may do them. That is the purpose for which we were created. In a book I read once, a story was told of a Christian woman who saw a homeless girl out in the cold and shivering in a thin dress. She looked limp and weak from hunger. The woman prayed, "Dear God, why don't You do something to help that little girl and others like her?" God replied, "I did do something—I made you!"

There is an interesting thought attached to the end of Ephesians 2:10 that I am afraid sometimes we may overlook. Notice it says we are "created in Christ Jesus to do good works, *which God prepared in advance for us to do.*" What does that mean? How in the world can good works be said to exist in advance of their being done? I like the way I heard someone explain it once: "The good works were already there (already thought up by God)."

Here is an example that helps me understand it. At Christmas time every year, the congregation where we worship prepares fruit baskets for all our elderly and shut-ins. One of the deacons buys fresh apples, oranges, and bananas, and the ladies make all kinds of cookies and good-ies. We usually meet on a Sunday afternoon and assemble the goods in festive containers. In the past, after completing them, we would each take a few of the baskets and deliver them. The last few years, however, we have tried something new. A lot of our young children are involved in a special service project called "Good Samaritans," which gives them the opportunity to earn points by doing acts of kindnesses. So we have started letting the children give out the baskets. A deacon loads them all up on the church van, drives to the different residences, and sends a child in with a big basket and a big smile. Now are these little ones actually responsible for the creation of the fruit baskets? No. But through their hands, our work is carried out. That's how it is with God; He works *through* us. In Acts 19:11, we read that God worked unusual miracles "by the hands of Paul" (KJV). I think the same thing happens today (not the miraculous part, of course, since miracles as such ceased after the first century). But good things are still accomplished by God, using the hands of His children.

(3) *To live as children of light means a deflection of glory.* Notice the con-cluding part of Matthew 5:16: "Let your light so shine before men, that they may see your good works, *and glorify your Father which is in heaven*" (KJV).

The purpose of the good works we do as children of light is never to claim recognition for ourselves, but rather to bring glory to God, the Father.

In 1 Peter 4, the apostle Peter mentions the different gifts and min-istries Christians have as stewards of God, and Paul comments that the purpose of each is "that God in all things, may be glorified" (verse 11).

When my children were young, I tried to tell them that the things they did before others—or did not do—was a reflection on me as their parent. I remember once at a birthday party instructing my daughter to get out of the swimming pool because it was time for us to leave. When she immediately complied, I found it interesting that a fellow parent (whose child was begging, alternately, for either "one more dive" or "five more minutes") complimented, not my daughter, but me for her obedience.

"She's a good little girl," I replied, nodding toward my daughter (and resisting the impulse to add, "most of the time!")

"She's good because of you," my friend replied.

Any goodness others see in us is because of God. He is the One who has made the difference in our lives.

As recorded in Acts 4, shortly after the establishment of the church, Peter and John were taken into custody for healing a lame man in the temple.

> *Any goodness others see in us is because of God. He is the One who has made the difference in our lives.*

When they appeared before Annas and Caiaphas the next day and presented their defense, the Jewish leaders are said to have "marvelled" (verse 13, NKJV).

These were lowly fishermen, remember: simple, uneducated men. As far as we know, nothing they had ever been or done before in their lives was particularly noteworthy.

When they exhibited uncharacteristic boldness, however, the rulers and scribes were "astonished" and "took note that these men had been with Jesus."

Anything we are, anything we do is never a credit to ourselves. It is because of whose we are . . . and the One with whom we have been.

MAKING A DIFFERENCE

One of many so-called urban legends that made the rounds recently on the Internet was a news report that actually appeared in the Birmingham, England *Sunday Mercury* on December 7, 2000.

The article had to do with a publishing firm employee who supposedly sat at his desk, dead for five days before anyone noticed!

The 51-year-old proofreader, George Turklebaum, had been an employee with the company 30 years. According to the newspaper, he passed away quietly on a Monday after suffering a coronary, but wasn't discovered until the following Saturday when someone on the cleaning staff stopped by and asked why he was working on the weekend.

The incident—later proven to be a complete fabrication!—still raises an interesting question. If something happened to me, would I be missed? Certainly, we all hope we would be missed. We like to think that we make a difference in the lives of those around us.

> What things do you hope that family, friends, and associates will miss about you after you are gone?
>
> _____
>
> _____
>
> _____

One person who certainly made a difference to her community was a Christian woman in Joppa named Dorcas. Upon her death, recorded in Acts 9, some of the disciples sent sent for Peter who was staying in the nearby city of Lydda. When Peter arrived at the house where Dorcas' body lay, he was met by a group of widows who had come to weep for her. They showed Peter the tunics and garments Dorcas had made for them.

One of my favorite cartoon strips is *Family Circle* by Bil Keane. In one classic, the mom is seen reading the following quotation from a book: "You will be remembered by what you leave behind," while young Billy enters the

> *One person who certainly made a difference in her community was . . . Dorcas.*

front door, leaving behind him a trail of miscellaneous items, including clothing, toys, and papers.

As we come and go throughout our daily activities, are we leaving behind us a trail of light?

WRITTEN ALL OVER US

Several years ago, our family had gone out of town for a soccer tournament. (Yes, I am one of *those* soccer moms!) My husband had packed a brand-new pair of jeans. They were so new, in fact, he had not even removed the tags yet. The following morning in the hotel, he got up and decided he would wear them. He took off the price tag, put them on, and went downstairs to the lobby for a continental breakfast. While he was getting his food, the mom of another player on our team, one of our friends, came up to him and smiled. "I like your new jeans, Roger, "she said.

"Thanks," he replied. "How did you know they were new?"

She pointed to the long stick-on plastic strip down the side of one leg, which read "36-32, 36-32, 36-32" for all the world to see! (Needless to say, this probably was not as traumatic for a man as it would have been for a woman!)

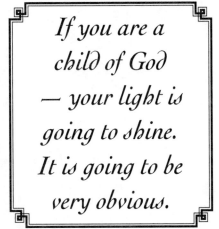

If you are a child of God — your light is going to shine. It is going to be very obvious.

But Roger's embarrassing incident illustrates an important principle. If you are a child of God, your light is going to shine. It is going to be very obvious; it is going to show. You will not have to walk around constantly de-claring, "I'm a Christian." People will know just by observing everything you do. *It will be written all over you.*

SUMMARY

As children of God, we are to be a reflection of His light to the world of darkness around us. This means we are to model the qualities of the Father for those with whom we come in contact. The impact He has had on us is something we will not be able to hide—and should not want to hide, even if we could.

Those whose lights shine to others will have put aside the "old man" and will focus now on striving for goodness. All of this is done, of course, with the goal of bringing glory to the Father.

CHAPTER 5

Walking in the Light

When our family lived in Brazil during the 1980's, I was amazed at the number of people who got to where they needed to go by walking. Sure, some people had cars (though not nearly as many as in the States). And a lively assortment of city buses, taxicabs, motorcycles, even animals, vied for space on crowded downtown streets. Still, the predominant mode of transportation was feet.

The same is true in other parts of the world, I am told. In fact, my aunt, a native of Wales, said when her sister came to the States from England for a visit and was given a tour of our town, her first question was, "Where are all the people?"

In most U.S. cities—with the exception of our large, metropolitan areas—you will not find throngs of people in the streets as you do in other countries.

> *Walking has been delegated to a pastime, a recreational sport.*

No, we Americans have discovered speedier ways to get around in our day-to-day existence. For us, walking has been delegated to a pastime, a recreational sport.

Unfortunately, the same can often be said of the Christian walk. Rather than being a way of life, it has become something many "do" only on occasion.

THE BIBLICAL CONCEPT OF WALKING

The word "walk" in the Bible implies much more than a way to get from here to there. In many cases, it refers to a relationship. Micah 6:8 says, "And what does the Lord require of you? To act justly and to love mercy and to walk humbly with your God."

Before his death, the great Israelite leader Moses challenged his people, "to love the Lord your God, to walk in his ways, and to keep his commands" (Deuteronomy 30:16).

In 1 Samuel 8 we see an example where a failure to walk is synonymous with rejection. Verses one and two tell us that when Samuel became old, he appointed his sons, Joel and Abijah, as judges over the people. "But his sons did not walk in his ways" (verse 3).

A similar idea is expressed in Jeremiah 6:16 where God says to His people, "Stand at the crossroads and look; ask for the ancient paths, ask where the good way is, and walk in it, and you will find rest for your souls." But the people replied, "We will not walk in it."

God's reaction to such a rebuff is evident in Psalm 81:13 where He laments with sadness, "Oh, that my people would listen to me, that Israel would walk in my ways!" (NKJV).

Jeremiah 7:6 speaks of those who "walk after other gods," and Jeremiah 18:12 of ones who walk according to their own plans (NKJV). In the New Testament, Peter refers to some who "walk after the flesh" (2 Peter 2:10, ASV), while Jude alludes to the ones who "would walk according to their own ungodly lusts" (Jude 1:18, NKJV).

> *"Oh, that my people . . . would walk in my ways!"*
> — *Psalm 81:13, NKJV*

The true desire of all, of course, should be to walk with the Lord, dressed in white, as is said of some in the church at Sardis (Revelation 3:4).

IN THE LIGHT OF HIS PRESENCE

Psalm 89:15 says, "Blessed are those who have learned to acclaim you, who walk in the light of your presence, O Lord."

> *"[L]et us walk in the light of the Lord."*
> — *Isaiah 2:5*

"Come, O house of Jacob," we read in Isaiah 2:5, "let us walk in the light of the Lord."

Further in the book of Isaiah, we read of some who walk in the light of their own fires and provide themselves with "flaming torches" that they have set ablaze (Isaiah 50:11). These, Isaiah says, are destined for torment.

What, we may wonder, was their mistake? Obviously, it was not the fact that they had found themselves in darkness, but that they tried to find their own solution. Notice the previous verse: "Let him who walks in the dark, who has no light, trust in the name of the Lord and rely on his God" (Isaiah 50:10).

So often we are guilty of trying to do things for ourselves or "help God." I am reminded of a poem I saw on a plaque in a gift shop. It said:

> My little girl helped me shell beans today,
> She kept the hulls and threw the beans away.
> I think sometimes that's how it must be
> When I try to help God the way she helps me.

Trying to find our own solutions is tempting to us at times. David A. Sargent in his Atwood Church of Christ bulletin (August 17, 2003) tells the story of Charles Proteus Steinmetz. A diminutive hunchback and a dwarf, Steinmetz lived from 1865 to 1923 and was one of the greatest minds the world has ever seen in the field of electricity. He came to the United States from Germany in 1889 as a political refugee and was hired by the General Electric Company in Schenectady, New York.

Steinmetz was the engineer who designed the massive turbine generators used by General Electric. In 1902, however, he retired and accepted a position to teach electrical engineering at Union College.

Once, after his retirement, the turbine generators that Steinmetz had designed broke down, leaving the entire GE plant in darkness. Needless to say, company officials were eager to solve the problem. They brought in all kinds of mechanics and technicians, but their efforts to repair the generators were unsuccessful. Finally, the plant manager called Steinmetz. He came in, puttered about for a short amount of time, and then threw the switch. The lights blinked, the turbines started up, and General Electric was back in business.

Shortly thereafter, the company received a bill for $10,000 from Steinmetz. Plant officials were stunned at the charge. They sent the engineer a note asking, "Charlie, isn't this bill just a little high for a few hours of *tinkering around* on those motors?"

A few days later, General Electric received another bill from Steinmetz. The bill had been adjusted and read as follows:

> For tinkering around on the motors — $1
> For knowing where to tinker — <u>$9,999</u>
> Total: $10,000

When you and I find ourselves in darkness, we don't need to try to come up with our own remedy. We need to call in the expert, the One who made us. He has the expertise and will not leave us in the dark

Think of a time in your life when you tried to solve a problem on your own, without consulting God or His Word. What was the result?

_____

_____

_____

JOHN'S DISCUSSION OF WALKING IN THE LIGHT

The idea of walking in the light is also mentioned at length in the book of 1 John.

There—specifically in verses five through seven of chapter one—John contrasts a walk of light with a walk of darkness.

SOME BACKGROUND

One of the first things you want to know when buying a house is "What is the neighborhood like?" Surroundings can tell you a lot about something. The same is true when we go to study the Bible. We don't ever need to pull out just a verse or two and read them alone—we need to check out the "neighborhood." That means, of course, that we should look at the context. Find out what is happening in the setting. Ask ourselves who is speaking—and to whom the comments are addressed. If we will do that, then the passage will be easier to understand, as well as much more meaningful.

> *"[Y]ou may know that you have eternal life."*
> *— 1 John 5:13*

The theme of 1 John, one of three epistles written by the apostle, is assurance. Why did John pen this letter? He tells us in chapter five that his purpose in writing is that "you" (Christians at that time, as well as those of us who live today) may *know* that you have eternal life (verse 13).

Don't you like to know things, to be sure of them? Is there a differ-ence in receiving a letter from Publishers Clearinghouse that says, "You *may* be a winner. . . " and having a representative show up on your door-step with a camera crew and a check for thousands of dollars? Of course there is! One is a remote possibility (of which we are actually rather doubtful), while the other is a life-changing reality.

John seems to be saying, here is something you can be sure of. In fact, if he were still living today, I have no doubt that one of his favorite songs would probably be the much-loved old hymn "Blessed Assurance." The message it conveys and the thoughts expressed in John's letter are very similar.

"Ab-so-for-sure-lute-ly"

The story is told of a man who had a young grandson who was very bright. (I know. *All* grandparents would make that same claim, right?) This little fellow, though, while only four years old, already had quite a way with words.

The lad also loved to fish. His grandfather would take him fishing quite often; it was a very special experience the two of them shared.

One evening, the grandfather asked the little boy, "Do you want to go fishing tomorrow?"

The child, eyes glistening with excitement, replied, "Yes, Grandpa!"

Deciding to tease him a bit, the grandfather asked, "Are you *sure* you want to go fishing tomorrow?"

The boy answered, "Yes, I'm sure, Grandpa!"

Enjoying the game, the grandfather then asked, "How sure are you that you want us to go fishing tomorrow?"

The four-year-old answered—with a word of his own creation—"Ab-so-for-sure-lute-ly!"

There are things about which we need to have that kind of confidence. Let's note what some of these things are.

(1) We can be sure of God. When I was a teenager, I loved to read poetry by Rod McKuen. One of his most famous poems was entitled "The Sea." It began:

How can we be sure of anything?
The tide changes, the wind that made the grain wave gently yesterday,
blows down trees tomorrow.
And the sea sends sailors crashing on the rocks as easily as it guides them home safely.

Change, at times, does seem to be everywhere around us. But there is one thing that changes not, and that is God.

The Psalmist writes in chapter 46 that because of God's stability, "we will not fear, though the earth give way and the mountains fall into the heart of the sea, though its waters roar and foam and the mountains quake with their surging. . . " (verses 2-3). No matter what else around us may change, He does not.

List some changes that have come about in the span of your lifetime.

_____

_____

_____

Paul Harvey, in one of his radio broadcasts, reported that with the naked eye 5,000 stars can be seen in the sky. However, there are actually some 70,000,000,000,000,000,000,000,000 stars in existence! (Try to pronounce *that* number!) Of all of these, of course, only one—the North Star—is constant. That is why sailors use it as their guide.

God is constant. "I the Lord do not change," He says in Malachi 3:6. What security we have when we look to Him for guidance!

> "I the Lord do not change."
> — Malachi 3:6

(2) *We can be sure of God's Word.* If our relationship with God were based only on feelings, there would be a lot of confusion. One person may feel one thing, while another feels something totally different altogether.

I heard a story that made quite an impression on me. The story is about a man who received a phone call telling him that his mother had passed away. The man lived in a different state, and someone who was at the hospital when his mother died made the phone call to inform him. Naturally, the son quickly made arrangements and caught the next plane home. He said that the entire time he was traveling, he was grief-stricken, mourning the loss of his dear mother.

When he arrived in his hometown, he called for someone to pick him up at the airport. Only then did he learn that the information he had received was false—his mother was not dead at all! Her heart had stopped, yes; and when it did, a well-meaning relative had left her bedside, walked down the hall, and placed the phone call to him. But when the relative returned to the room, he found that the hospital staff had been able to revive the woman! He quickly hurried back to the phone to report this development, but there was no answer because the man had already left his home for the airport.

The son was able to spend the next several days at his mother's bedside. Unfortunately, however, less than a week later, she did pass away.

Once again, the man was filled with a sense of sadness and grief, exactly the same kind of sorrow he had experienced on his journey home. There was no difference at all, he said, except for one thing: one feeling was based on truth while the other had been based on error.

What a blessing it is for us to have God's Word, the truth! Our relationship with Him does not have to be based on feelings, but rather on things that are written down—the holy, inspired, and unchanging scriptures.

(3) We can be sure of our salvation.

One of my college professors once described for our class the last days of his father's life. His father, mind you, had been a Christian for many, many years, the biggest portion of his life, in fact. Nevertheless, on his deathbed—according to his son—the elderly gentleman was still doubtful of his salvation. Oh, he *hoped* he had lived a good enough life, he *hoped* he would go to heaven, but there was no assurance. Hearing him with such uncertainty in his heart made my professor very sad.

When it comes time for us to die—and not just then, but also while we are living!—we can be confident about the promises of God. We don't have to say, "Well, I *hope*. . ." We can know, John says, and know assuredly! What peace that gives us.

What impact will being sure of your salvation have on your attitude toward death?

_____

_____

_____

THE HUMAN FLY

Years ago, there was a traveling entertainer who billed himself as "The Human Fly." He would climb up the sides of buildings and monuments, without using any ropes and without having any nets to protect him.

During one performance, he came to a certain point on the wall, and then reached out with his right hand to grab a piece of mortar to lift himself higher. But instead, he fell back with a scream and was killed on the pavement below.

When the police came to remove his body, they opened up his right hand. Instead of mortar inside, guess what they found? A handful of dirty cobwebs!

Occasionally there may be cobwebs in my house that look pretty sturdy—they have been there so long!—but we all know you can't support yourself with something that is not solid.

Yet how many times do we try to hang onto things as unsubstantial as cobwebs? Money, material possessions, human relationships—all of these are subject to change. They are iffy, not guaranteed.

> *Jesus Christ is the same "yesterday and today and forever."*
> — *Hebrews 13:8*

The only sure thing we can hang onto is Jesus Christ, who is the same "yesterday and today and forever" (Hebrews 13:8).

I love the story of a kindergarten class that went on a field trip to the local police station one day. While there, they saw pictures, tacked to a bulletin board, of the ten most wanted men in the state.

One of the youngsters pointed to a particular picture and asked if it was really the photograph of a criminal.

"Yes," replied the police chief. "He's done some terrible things. The detectives want him very badly."

Little Johnny then said, "Well, why didn't you just keep him when you took his picture?"

We need to hold on to the things that we have, don't we? And what we have, John reminds us in the book of 1 John, is eternal life. We are assured of it, he says, as long as we walk in the light.

FORWARD MOTION

Kids have a knack for putting some lofty ideas into very simple phrases. For example, one little girl defined the word "walk" this way: "to get past where you were when you first started."

Now, granted, that is not a very scientific definition, but it goes right along with what John is talking about in 1 John 1:7. As Christians, if we walk in the light, we are going to move forward, implying growth and progress.

Sometimes on televised football games, I hear a penalty announced for something called "forward motion." Apparently, it is illegal for a lineman or a wide receiver to advance beyond the line of scrimmage before the ball is snapped.

In the Christian life, however, forward motion is not only permitted, it is essential.

Each day that I live my new life in Christ, I need to know a little more, love a little more, and become just a little bit stronger.

Ask yourself: Am I past where I was when I first started my life as a Christian? Am I further along than I was five years ago, one year ago, six months ago?

I should be.

Proverbs 4:18 tells us, "The path of the righteous is like the first gleam of dawn, shining ever brighter till the full light of day."

I like the way Kenneth Taylor paraphrased this passage in *Living Psalms and Proverbs with the Major Prophets*: "But the good man walks along in the *ever brightening light* of God's favor; the dawn gives way to morning splendor" (emphasis mine).

The further along we advance in our Christian walk, the longer we have been with our Lord, the brighter His light in our lives should become.

What are some specific growths you can see in yourself since first becoming a Christian? In what areas do you still need to improve?

_____

_____

_____

_____

Summary

Our relationship with God is often described in the Bible as "walking in the light."

This implies or suggests several different concepts.

First, we should look to God to provide light instead of trying to find our own solutions to the darkness.

Second, this walk should fill us with confidence or assurance.

Thirdly, our walk should be a progression. The longer we continue our journey together, God's light should become ever brighter in our lives.

CHAPTER 6

Staying in the Circle: Communion

A woman in the country of India was walking to her home late one evening. As she went, she became aware that she was being followed. Looking back over her shoulder, she realized that there was a panther on her heels!

Undaunted, she did not overreact. Instead, she merely continued at her normal pace and was able to arrive safely at her destination.

How did she manage to escape harm? According to the woman, it was because she was carrying a lantern and walked within the circle of its brightness.

"A panther," she explained, "will not attack you while you are in the light."

Having attempted to trace the roots of this story—without success, I regret to say—I am unable to verify its authenticity. But I find the concept fascinating, at least when applied to the Biblical idea of walking in the light.

Within the circle of God's light, there are numerous blessings. The first one we want to consider is communion with Him.

NEVER ALONE

Notice the first part of 1 John 1:7: "if we walk in the light, *as he is in the light. . .*" (emphasis mine). As we walk along, God is there with us, isn't He? Our walk is with Him; therefore, we are not alone.

Charles L. Allen, in his book *You Are Never Alone*, quotes a poem by Joyce Kilmer, entitled "The House With Nobody In It."

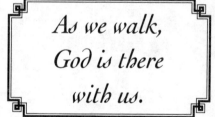

As we walk, God is there with us.

> Whenever I walk to Suffern, along the Erie track
> I go by a poor old farmhouse with its shingles broken and black.
> I suppose I've passed it a hundred times
> But I always stop for a minute
> And look at that house, the tragic house,
> The house with nobody in it.

I've never seen a haunted house,
But I hear there are such things;
That they hold the talk of spirits,
Their mirth and their sorrowings.
I know this house isn't haunted,
But I wish it were; I do;
For it wouldn't be so lonely
If it had a spirit or two.

If I had a lot of money
And all my debts were paid,
I'd put a gang of men to work,
With brush and saw and spade.
I'd buy that place
And I'd fix it up the way it used to be
And I'd find some people who wanted a house
And I'd give it to them, for free.

So whenever I go to Suffern,
Along the Erie track,
I never go by that empty house
Without stopping and looking back.
It hurts me to look at the crumbling roof
And the shutters falling apart,
For I can't help thinking the poor old house
Is a house with a broken heart.

"There is a tragedy in emptiness and many people who are living alone feel it," Allen writes. "Being by yourself oftentimes is like living in a house with nobody in it."

Jesus certainly knew the bleakness of being alone. In Mark 14, on the eve of the crucifixion, we read of His lonely vigil in the Garden of Gethsemane. Though He was noticeably "distressed and troubled" (verse 33) and even confided to His companions that He felt "overwhelmed with sorrow" (verse 34), they selfishly fell asleep and provided Him no solace.

A few hours later, when Judas led a group into the garden to arrest Him, we are told, "all the disciples deserted him and fled" (Matthew 26:56). Of course, the ultimate cry of loneliness echoed from the cross itself: "My God, my God, why have *you* forsaken me?" (Matthew 27:46, emphasis mine).

We do not have to worry about ever being forsaken by God. Even if earthly friends may leave, as long as we walk in the light, He is going to be there beside us.

Name a circumstance in which you felt overcome with loneliness. How does it make you feel to know that Jesus dealt with something very similar?

_____

_____

_____

THE EXAMPLE OF ENOCH

Whenever I think of someone walking with God, the first person who comes to my mind is Enoch. What a beautiful relationship the two of them must have shared—so intimate, in fact, that God did not want to leave him down on this earth any longer and just took him home with Him to live. Why? Hebrews 11:5 says because Enoch "pleased God."

This story—one we can read in Genesis 5—makes me think of something that happened back when I was in elementary school. After worship, on summer nights especially, a friend and I would always play together outdoors after services while the grownups were visiting. We would enjoy it so much that whenever it was time to leave, I would say to my friend's mom (or she would say to mine), "Can't she *please* just go home with me?"

I imagine a similar scene: God and Enoch together, having such a good time (we do not often think of God in those terms, do we?), their relationship so close that God says, "Just go home with me, Enoch." And Enoch went.

There are a couple of sidelights to this story that are worthy of our consideration.

What impresses you most about the relationship between God and Enoch? Can you see any differences in your own relationship with God? Any similarities?

_____

_____

_____

One is the fact (verified by Jude in verse 14 . . . or you can count it yourself in Genesis!) that Enoch was the seventh generation from Adam. I do not know if that is just a coincidence or not (it well may be), but oftentimes in the Bible the number seven stands for completeness. Enoch certainly was complete in his devotion to God. His life was wholly dedicated to his maker.

Genesis 5, where Enoch is mentioned, is a most unique chapter. It basically lists the genealogy and ages of all the patriarchs. Verse 23 tells us how old Enoch was when he was taken away into heaven—365 years old. There again, it

> *Enoch certainly was complete in his devotion to God.*

may be just a coincidence, but I find it interesting that his age is the same as the number of days in a year. This could be viewed as another symbolism for wholeness.

Something else to note is that eight times in chapter five, after the listing of the name of an individual and his age, you will find the words, "and he died." James Burton Coffman, in his commentary on Genesis, says this emphasizes the "reign of death" during the long journey of Adam's fallen race.   He adds, "What a brutal lie the glib denial of Satan turned out to be!" (Remember how he told Eve, "You will *not* surely die"? Genesis 3:4, emphasis mine).

Suddenly, though, right there, exactly at the halfway point between Adam and the Flood is an event that defies all the dying. The translation of Enoch gives a promise of something else—life, life *eternal!*—to all the descendants. It is like a reminder from God: *This death thing does not have to be permanent! I have other plans! If you will love Me and serve Me with your whole being—like Enoch—then I will make it possible for you to come live with Me forever. Just like him.*

Just like Enoch. Wow. There is an example worthy of being followed!

ENOCH'S FAMOUS SON

Most of us have probably heard of Enoch's son, Methuselah, who has the distinction of being the oldest man who ever lived. Methuselah died at the very ripe old age of 969 and, interestingly enough, passed away in the year of the flood. (Does that mean he actually died *in* the flood? Some think so.)

Commentators also draw attention to the notation in Genesis 5:22 that Enoch walked with God *after* he begat Methuselah, suggesting that before the birth of his son he had not done so. Was that the case? Again, the Bible does not tell us. But certainly if it were, Enoch would not be the first to resolve to live a more godly life after becoming a parent. Having a child is a tremendous responsibility and should cause all of us to re-think our goals, aspirations, and priorities.

Another lesson this could teach us—if Enoch did delay his obedience to God—is that it is never too late in life to make a good decision. Regardless of when he started his walk, we know the difference it made in Enoch. No matter what he had done before, after becoming a father, Enoch spent time *with* the Father.

> *It is never too late in life to make a good decision.*

OTHERS WHO WALKED WITH GOD

You realize, I am sure, that Enoch was not the first to have walked with God. Back in Paradise, it happened all the time. God would come down in the cool of the evening to the lovely garden He had made and walk with His creation.

What a special time it must have been! This was the companionship that God had craved, the very reason He had decided to make man in the first place.

Something changed all that, though. Sin entered the world, and man removed himself and hid from his Maker.

Fortunately, we no longer have to be estranged. Thanks to Jesus, we have been brought back to where we can once again walk with God.

After Enoch, only one other character in the Bible is said to have walked with God. Oh, there were others who walked before Him. Solomon, describing his father David, verifies, "he walked before You in truth, in righteousness, in uprightness of heart" (1 Kings 3:6, NKJV). Hezekiah, when he was sick and near the point of death, pleaded with the Lord, asking Him to remember "how I have walked before thee in truth and with a perfect heart" (2 Kings 20:3, KJV). And sometimes the phrase "walk after" is used to describe someone who followed the Lord (Deuteronomy 13:4, KJV).

> *Enoch was not the first to have walked with God. Back in Paradise it happened all the time.*

But only Noah (Genesis 6:9) is said to have "walked with God" as did Enoch. And, in a phrase similar to the Hebrew writer's statement that Enoch "pleased God" (Hebrews 11:5), we read that Noah "found favor" with the Lord (Genesis 6:8).

What do you think Noah might have done that brought a smile to the lips of the Almighty?

(1) Noah lived a life that was in contrast to the lives of those around him. During Noah's days, the earth was "corrupt" and "full of violence" (Genesis 6:11). You get the impression that the same kind of things making headlines today could well have been happening then. God was "grieved" over this turn of events; His heart, Moses records, was "filled with pain" (Genesis 6:6). But there was one person who did not "follow the crowd in doing wrong" (Exodus 23:2). Noah apparently stood his ground and refused to be influenced by the conduct of all those around him.

(2) Noah spoke up for his beliefs. In 2 Peter 2:5, Noah is called a "preacher of righteousness." Apparently he (as well as Enoch—see Jude 14-15) very aggressively testified to unbelievers in his midst. One can only imagine the

ridicule and scorn he doubtlessly had to endure. Boat jokes were probably a dime a dozen, but more than likely the laughter began to ebb just about the time the raindrops started to fall.

(3) Noah had a positive influence on his family. While Noah made no headway in convincing his neighbors and friends of the impending doom, he was still able to secure the salvation of his own household. This (something that Lot, for example, was unable to do—see Genesis 19:14) is no small feat.

> What things do I do that might bring a smile to the lips of the Almighty?
>
> _____
>
> _____
>
> _____

COMMUNION WITH GOD TODAY

In Psalm 4:4, we are told, "Stand in awe, . . . commune with your own heart upon your bed, and be still" (KVJ).

Stillness is something that is practically nonexistent in our society today. From the moment we wake up in the morning, we are on the go, flying around at breakneck speed from one activity to another. In fact, in a world where *doing* is glorified, inactivity often has a negative connotation and is equated with laziness.

The popular country singing group, *Alabama,* summed it up well with their 1993 hit, *I'm In A Hurry.*

> I'm in a hurry to get things done
> Oh, I rush and rush until life's no fun
> All I really gotta do is live and die
> But I'm in a hurry and don't know why.

In order to have an intimate relationship with God, time for quietness and reflection is a must.

"Be still," Psalm 46:10 instructs us, "and know that I am God."

In the Old Testament, God had a period designed specifically for contemplation that was built into the Jewish lifestyle. Their forced "day off" was the Sabbath—a term that literally means *rest*. Just as God had rested after His labor at the beginning of time when He created the world (Genesis 2:2), man was instructed to refrain from physical work and enjoy a period of both physical and spiritual refreshment.

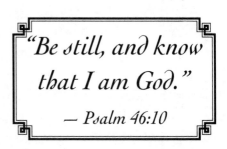

"Be still, and know that I am God."

— *Psalm 46:10*

Rick Atchley, in his book *Sinai Summit: Meeting God With Our Character Crisis*, notes that while work was part of God's original plan and something He highly approves, He probably realized that man would often take work to the extreme, and so He made a command for us to rest. Just as little children will fight sleep, all the while insisting that they are not tired, adults often forego much-needed periods of respite. Perhaps, Atchley muses, this explains the terminology of the much-loved Psalm 23: "He *maketh* me to lie down in green pastures. . ." (verse 2, KJV).

We need to make time in our busy lives to commune with the Father. How can we do this?

(1) Meditate, pray, and study. Set aside a period each day for meditation, prayer, and Bible study. It may help you to establish a routine if you do this at the same time every day, but that is not essential. Schedules change, so it is important that you learn to be flexible.

(2) Clear your mind. Instead of rushing right into a prayer or reading scripture, pause first and clear your mind. It may help to close your eyes and focus on a serene setting. Imagine yourself at a deserted beach or in the mountains, somewhere far away from your actual surroundings.

(3) Worship. Too often we think of worship merely as something we do in a church pew. One definition, however, is "to regard with extravagant respect or devotion," and you can do that anywhere! Concentrate on the marvels of creation and the power of the deity who made them. (*Please note*: This may not come easily. For too long, in our time with the Lord, the focus has been on *us* and our needs. That is not how it should be! To aid you in this area, it may help to read from Psalms or even softly recite the words of a hymn. Praise God for being God. Make a mental list—or write it down if you prefer—of His qualities or all the things He has done.)

(4) Confess. From a period of praise, you will evolve quite naturally into a period of confession. After acknowledging the goodness and the greatness of God, turn inward for a moment and take a look at yourself. Doubtless, you will be stunned by the contrast. All the emphasis on self-image in recent times may have made us inclined to downplay our inadequacies so that we can better "like" ourselves. But it is important to take a honest look. Examination of weaknesses and shortcomings brings to Light our need for and dependence upon God's grace.

(5) Express gratitude. We often smile at a young child's tendency to enumerate everything in eyesight during a prayer. One of my all-time favorites came from the lips of a four-year-old and was recorded by his preschool teacher:

> *Dear God,*
> Thank you for Jesus and for the church.
> Thank you for our head and our face.
> Thank you for our eyes to see birds and shoot and kill them.
> Thank you for our shoulders and shoulder pads and tackles
>   and rebounds.
> Thank you for healthy bodies and legs to run fast and play
>   baseball and run to bases.
> And thank you for our mommies and daddies and teachers.
> Thank you for our supper and our plates.
> Thank you for our skin to hold us together.
> And thank you for our bodies to hold up our heads.
> In Jesus' name,
> *Amen*

Unfortunately, as adults, we tend to lose some of that wide-eyed wonder and start lumping all our blessings together under a blanket statement, thanking God for "everything." Try to avoid that. Get back to specifics, making sure you mention things spiritual as well as physical.

(6) Spend time in God's Word. Read not just for factual knowledge, nor for encouragement (though, hopefully, both will be a by-product of your reading). I have never forgotten what I heard a preacher say once at a workshop: "In every text I read, I should ask myself, 'What do I see in this that requires me to change?'"

What things in today's society make it difficult to be still and rest? How can you combat current lifestyles to make sure you have enough time for meditation and reflection? _____

_____

_____

_____

Write a prayer of praise to God.

_____

_____

_____

Write a prayer of confession.

_____

_____

_____

Write a prayer of gratitude.

_____

_____

_____

SUMMARY

One of the wonderful things about walking in the Light is the benefit of having communion with God. He is there with us each step of the way. Just as some of our Old Testament heroes (Enoch, Noah) are said to have walked with God, we can experience togetherness with Him today if we will but take the time and make the effort. We know God wants it; He longs for it, in fact. Question is: do *we* desire it?

CHAPTER 7

Staying in the Circle:

Obedience

When I was in the seventh grade, I had my first "serious" boyfriend. Back then, "serious" (in junior high terms) implied certain things: we talked on the phone occasionally, he gave me his basketball sweater to wear, and I lettered his name all over my notebooks. Once or twice, as I recall, we even met somewhere like a park or fair (with other friends, of course). More than anything else, though, it meant that we walked together at school.

The building that housed our classrooms was square. At the center of it was an auditorium, and around the outer edge were similarly-sized cubicles in which we daily studied English, math, science, and history. Between the classrooms and the area for general assemblies was a hallway. Every morning upon arrival at school, students hurriedly deposited their books in homeroom and then circled the halls, chatting with friends until time for the bell to ring. The unwritten rule was that "couples" always walked together.

At lunch time, it was more of the same. In those days (weather permitting), we could leave the cafeteria when we finished eating and walk around the campus until time to return to class. You always knew a new romance was brewing if you saw a girl get up from her lunch table of girlfriends and head outside with a member of the opposite sex. Of course, the opposite was true as well. If a twosome was seen walking in groups of their friends instead of with one another, then obviously there was trouble in paradise.

> *"Can two walk together, except they be agreed?"*
> — *Amos 3:3, KJV*

It was the manifestation of an age-old truth, worded so appropriately in Amos 3:3: "Can two walk together, except they be agreed?" (KJV).

WHAT WALKING WITH GOD INFERS

If I am walking with God, there are certain things that are implied. For one, it means I belong to Him. I am His, He is mine, and we are committed to one another. We are in a serious relationship.

A second implication is that I have accepted and met God's demands.

A good illustration of this is found in John 6. Not too long after the feeding of the five thousand, Jesus rebuked some of His disciples. He said they were only following Him in order to have their stomachs filled, when they should have been more interested in the bread of life. The people did not understand what He meant, calling it a "hard" saying. From that point on, according to verse 66, many turned away and "walked no more with him" (KJV).

Do I walk with God only for what I can get out of it, only for the benefits such a walk affords? Or do I continue at His side, even through periods of uncertainty, constantly yielding myself to the stipulations set forth?

> *Do I walk with God only for what I can get out of it?*

Surely, as Amos wrote, walking together denotes agreement. This, however, does not mean that I sit back and wait for God to nod acceptance of my chosen ways. Rather, I must be obedient to Him and His commands.

What are some wrong reasons that people follow Jesus today?

_____

_____

_____

_____

AN OLD TESTAMENT EXAMPLE

Throughout the first 39 books of the Bible, we see many cases where God emphasized the importance of obedience to His will. Under the old law, the Hebrew writer tells us in Hebrews 2:2, ". . . every violation and disobedience received its just punishment."

Nowhere is this made clearer to me than in a relatively little known (and even less understood) incident from 1 Kings 13: the story of the old and young prophet. While a somewhat lengthy and involved narrative, it is nevertheless worthy of our consideration.

BACKGROUND

The incident occurs at a time following the death of Solomon when the Hebrew kingdom was split. Jeroboam became the first king of the northern kingdom, which was comprised of the ten tribes of Israel. Unfortunately, it is said of Jeroboam: "he made Israel to sin" (an interesting choice of words!). Naturally, we understand that no one can force someone else to sin; that is a decision they themselves make. One can, however, lead them in the direction of sin, and that is exactly what Jeroboam did. He introduced digression from true worship by setting up golden bulls—one in Bethel and the other in Dan. The really sad part is that of the eighteen kings who ruled after him, we are told that fifteen "departed not" from the sin of Jeroboam. (Lesson to us today: Be careful what you do! You may be setting a precedent that will continue long after you are gone.)

In 1 Kings 13, Jeroboam, who had been king for only a short time, was preparing to dedicate the altar at Bethel. He was about to burn incense when God sent a prophet to him. This, to me, says how much God wants people to change, to stop before we are too far gone!

> What are some precedents that have been set in your family through the years?
>
> _____
>
> _____
>
> _____

DENUNCIATION OF THE IDOLATRY

Verse two tells us that the prophet "cried out," an expression that, according to Matthew Henry, denotes both courage and earnestness. The prophet was not ashamed to speak out—and speak out boldly—against wrongdoing. This boldness was one of the qualities of the early Christians (see Acts 4:31), and should also be a characteristic of Christians today.

It may seem a bit odd to us that the prophet addressed his comments to the altar, but in condemning it, he condemned all those associated with the pagan worship that would take place upon it. He also made a prophecy—one of the most remarkable and amazing in all the Old Testament because it foretells a very specific event that would take place 340 years after its prediction. The prophecy was that a future son of the house of David, named Josiah, would stand in exactly the same place Jeroboam was standing and would destroy the pagan practice. (Josiah, the young boy who became king at the tender age of eight, did that very thing in 2 Kings 23.)

Think of an incident from your life where you exhibited boldness.

_____

_____

_____

THE WITHERED HAND

We all know that in New Testament times, miracles accompanied the teaching of the gospel to prove it was from God. Sometimes, of course, the same thing happened with God's spokesmen in the Old Testament, and this was one of those instances. A miraculous occurrence accompanied the prophet's message: the altar was cracked, and ashes poured forth from it.

Jeroboam was displeased with the prophet's message, so (as often is the case), he decided to strike out against the messenger. But when he reached forth his hand and gave the command, "Seize him!" guess what happened? His hand basically froze in midair. He couldn't move it! It

> *The Word of God should have touched his conscience, but ... what got his attention was something affecting his fleshly body.*

withered. (Remember the man whose withered hand Jesus made whole in Matthew 12? That particular miracle is the second healing of a withered hand in scripture.)

At that point, Jeroboam begged the prophet to pray to God for him. Isn't he much like us? The Word of God should have touched his conscience, but it didn't. What got his attention was something that affected his fleshly body. Then—and only then—he cried out for help. In a similar way, so many of us do not turn to God until we suffer serious illness or the loss of a loved one. When that happens, however, all of a sudden we are ready to pray, ready to bargain.

It is also interesting to note the nature of Jeroboam's request. He did not ask the prophet to pray that his sin be forgiven or that his heart be changed—just that his hand be restored! (As always, still thinking only of the physical.)

The prayer was answered, though. God restored Jeroboam's hand. Perhaps God hoped to melt Jeroboam's heart with mercy (since obviously he was not motivated with the threat of judgment). And, at first, Jeroboam did seem to be touched. He asked the prophet to go home with him and eat, eager to reward him.

Look closely at the prophet's reply when Jeroboam extended his invitation (verses eight and nine); his reply was important to what happened next. Basically, the prophet responded, *No way! I wouldn't go with you even if you were to offer to give me half your kingdom.* Why was he so adamant? Because the Lord had implicitly forbidden him to eat bread and drink water there. In the East at that particular time in history, the extension of hospitality was a social obligation, a source of great honor and pride, and refusal to accept it was a very extreme action. God's prohibition, therefore, indicated His complete rejection of Jeroboam and Bethel. He abhorred what was going on and did not want His prophet to have any part of it.

List some places you think God would *not* want us to be? Why?

_____

_____

_____

_____

Not only had God forbidden the prophet to eat there, He had also told him to return home a different way than he had come. That was probably for his safety, as in the case of the wise men after their visit to the baby Jesus (Matthew 2:12). Some scholars have speculated that if people in surrounding areas heard what had happened in Bethel, they might have harassed the prophet on his way back through or might have delayed him from a prompt return.

THE OLD PROPHET'S DECEPTION

The next part of the story is what has often caused difficulty. Even to serious Bible students, it may seem a bit harsh and somewhat unfair.

Kings 13:11 says, "Now there was a certain old prophet living in Bethel. . . " When I used to read this, I always imagined someone rather advanced in years. The more I study the text, however, the more I am convinced that the reference may not have had anything to do with age. A better translation might be *a former prophet*, perhaps someone originally trained at one of Samuel's schools.

Despite what he had been in the past, however, most scholars agree that he certainly was not a man of God anymore. The spirit of prophecy had apparently departed from him (evidenced by the fact, in verse 18, that he lies). But also, had he been a good prophet, surely he would have been speaking out against Jeroboam's idolatry. Also, we are told in 2 Chronicles 11:16 that the truly devout Israelites—"such as set their hearts to seek the Lord God" (KJV)—had left their homes when Jeroboam made his religious changes and moved to Jerusalem. F. C. Cook says the fact that the old prophet remained under Jeroboam and was even content to dwell at Bethel (the chief seat of the new worship) tells us plenty about his religious standing.

The old prophet proceeded to pursue the man of God, and notice where he found him. Burton Coffman says: "It must be considered significant that the man of God was idly resting under an oak tree instead of returning to Judah; the man could not have been blameless because God had clearly instructed him to waste no time on his mission. Many another servant of God has been overcome with disaster in a moment of idleness."

Coffman also notes that while it is not actually stated, there appears to have been an unworthy desire on the part of the man of God to go back, and where there is willingness, there is always provided by Satan an opportune invitation to do wrong. (Remember how Jonah did not want to go to Nineveh and preach, so instead he went to Joppa and boarded a ship? I heard a preacher say once that Satan will always have a ship ready to take us far away from God.)

The old prophet invited the young prophet to come home with him, and once more, as he had done with the king, the young prophet repeats the instructions that he had received from God. But notice what the old prophet said in verse 18: The old prophet answered, "I too am a prophet, as you are. And an angel said to me by the word of the Lord: Bring him back with you to your house so that he may eat bread and drink water." *(But he was lying to him.)*

> *The fact that the old prophet remained under Jeroboam and was content to dwell at Bethel . . . tells us plenty about his religious standing.*

Why did the old prophet lie? Some commentators excuse the old prophet and say, *the old prophet had heard about what happened with Jeroboam and just wanted to hear a firsthand account,* or *that was just his way of getting the young prophet over to his house.* Others think the old prophet intentionally tripped up the man of God to undo the damage imposed earlier that day on the pagan religion. (False prophets, they argue, seek to draw true prophets away from their duty.) Either way, the man of God accepted the invitation. The saddest

What are some ways that God's people may be drawn away from their duties today?

_____

_____

_____

_____

part of the whole story for me is the fact that the young prophet believed him, went to his house and ate, and ended up dying as a result, killed by a lion as he departed (verse 24).

LESSONS

For years, many have struggled with this incident. How did the young prophet sin? they ask. Why did his sin cost him his life? He had obeyed God so faithfully up to that point, he had spoken out against evil as he had been instructed, and he had resisted the previous temptation to disobey. His only mistake was in believing what a fellow prophet said. Wouldn't we all have done the same?

We may have. But one of the lessons we can learn from this story—and there are many—is that not everyone who says he is a prophet really is a prophet. "Do not believe every spirit," John writes in 1 John 4:1, "but test the spirits to see whether they are from God." Worth noting also is the fact that the old prophet did not say God had spoken to him, he said an angel had spoken to him. That reminds me of Paul's statement in Galatians 1:8, "But even if we or an angel from heaven should preach a gospel other than the one we preached to you, let him be eternally condemned!"

God wants us to remain faithful to *His Word*—not to the word of religious leaders, not even to the word of angels were they to speak to us, and certainly not to the word of people who say that angels have spoken to them! (This story in and of itself, it seems to me, should make us very skeptical of dealing with those who claim to have talked with heavenly beings!)

Another fact to consider is that God does not change like "shifting shadows" (James 1:17), telling us one thing one minute and something totally different the next. Cook says, "If God gives a command and revokes it, He will revoke it as plainly and with as much evidence as He gave it. Here there was neither the same plainness, nor as strong evidence."

> *Serious consequences only serve to reiterate the serious nature of God's instructions.*

As far as the punishment goes: Yes, it does seem harsh, but so did that of Nadab and Abihu (Leviticus 10:1,2), and Ananias and Sapphira (Acts 5:1-11). Serious consequences only serve to reiterate the serious nature of God's instructions.

Ironically, the young prophet's downfall was exactly the same transgression as the one he had denounced only moments earlier with Jeroboam: disobedience to the command of God.

UNUSUAL DETAILS

Something odd occurred at the death of the young prophet. The lion that had attacked him stood by his body, but in contrast to its nature did not devour the corpse. Also, the donkey on which the prophet had been riding stood there as well, showing no fear of the lion, and the lion did not appear to take notice of the donkey. Both of those circumstances are highly unusual and show the miraculous nature of the death. Due to such unusual circumstances, attention was bound to have been called to the incident, and the story probably spread like wildfire through the people. By such a means, says Cook, an incident Jeroboam would have preferred hushed up no doubt became common knowledge among the people.

> Why would Jeroboam have wanted to keep quiet the things that happened? What kinds of reactions do you think people may have had upon hearing about the incident?
>
> _____
>
> _____
>
> _____

THE IMPACT

Many wonder if perhaps the old prophet was not changed because of what had transpired. In verse 29, he is no longer referred to as the "old" prophet, but rather simply "the prophet." He appears to have been filled with remorse that his shameful lie had led to the death of the young prophet. Coffman writes: "Whatever the reputation of this old prophet might have been in Bethel before the events of this chapter, he was forever afterwards enrolled among those prophesying the end of the regime of Jeroboam and religious systems represented by Bethel."

How could the old prophet have made up for what he did?

_____

_____

_____

_____

SUMMARY

An important part of walking with God involves not only commitment to a serious relationship with Him but acceptance of and adherence to His commands. Obedience, something even Jesus had to learn (Hebrews 5:8), is paramount in the prerequisites of Christianity.

The gospel of John tells us that some of Christ's followers turned away and ended their association with Him because they found His teachings to be difficult.

CHAPTER 8

Staying in the Circle: Fellowship

Several years ago, I went with my oldest son's drama class to a production of the play "To Kill A Mockingbird" in Nashville. We left from his high school early that morning, a caravan of three mini-vans filled with students. The lead van was driven by the class teacher—the only one, as it turned out, with directions to where we were going. Another parent drove the second van, and I brought up the rear.

The weather that day was horrendous. The closer we got to Nashville, the harder it rained, and the wipers on my aging vehicle were not getting the job done. I frantically leaned forward in my seat, straining to see through a foggy windshield, as eighteen-wheelers whizzed by on my left, dousing us in the process.

Had I been alone, there is no doubt in my mind I never would have made it to the theater. Thanks to my youthful companions, however, we succeeded. "They're getting off at the next exit, Mrs. Copeland," they informed me, as

> *Had I been alone . . . I never would have made it.*

I momentarily looked away, fiddling with my defroster. "You need to get in the right hand lane."

Then: "They're taking a left at the next intersection. I think the car behind us will let you over."

Later: "There's the sign for the theater up ahead. But the parking is going to be in the back."

Their assistance was invaluable. When I temporarily lost sight of the one I was following, they kept me on track. You see, we all had the same purpose: we all wanted to go to the same place. By helping one another, we were able to reach our destination.

That, in a nutshell, is what Christian fellowship is all about. Heaven is my goal, but if I had to get there on my own, would I make it? Absolutely not. I would get bogged down in difficulties of the journey; I would lose sight of the one guiding my way.

How blessed we are to have fellow travelers accompanying us!

In this chapter, we will examine one of the added benefits of walking in the light, the fact that, according to 1 John 1:7, "we have fellowship with one another."

"PIECE, PERFECT PIECE"

In 1995, I spoke at a ladies' retreat in Huntsville, Alabama. The topic they assigned me was "Piece, Perfect Piece," a clever play on words, emphasizing how Christians with different roles fit together in the church.

One of the objects used to illustrate the theme was a quilt. Individual believers, the retreat's coordinators explained, are like different blocks that God pieces together into one unit. I liked that comparison; after all, Paul tells us in Ephesians 2:10 that we are "God's workmanship." And in Psalm 139:15, where it talks about God creating us, the Hebrew word used is the same as that of a woman doing tedious embroidery. Quilts are lovely to behold, and serve a

> *Individual believers are like different blocks that God pieces together into one unit.*

useful purpose as well. (Shouldn't the same be said of God's people?)

Much as I enjoy beautiful bed coverings, however, I am not a quilter. Despite being the daughter of a very accomplished seamstress, I barely know one end of a needle from the other! So I could not relate to that example nearly as much as I could a second one used: a puzzle. (I have mothered four children, remember, so I have worked a lot of puzzles in my day!)

Think about some of the characteristics of puzzle pieces. No two are alike. They come in different sizes, different shapes, and different colors. Some puzzle pieces are plain, while others are very colorful. Some have smooth sides, but most are jagged. Now think for a minute about those of us who make up the church. Most all of these same things are also true of us. No two Christians are exactly alike. We have different shapes and sizes and are of different races as well. Some of us are a lot plainer than others, but we definitely have some colorful characters in our number! And while some brethren may be even-tempered, most of us are a bit rough around the edges.

One thing, however, is true of all puzzle pieces. They have protrusions and indentations. So do we as God's people. The indentations represent our weaknesses—our faults, limitations, and undeveloped areas. We all have those. The protrusions represent our strengths—our gifts, talents, and abilities. We all have those, too (whether we admit it or not!).

But the beautiful thing is, in the body of Christ, just like in a puzzle, my protrusions fill in your indentations, and your protrusions fill in mine. We complement one another. When just one puzzle piece is missing, its absence is very obvious, isn't it? In the same way, though, when everything is as it should be, in place, you don't notice the individual pieces so much anymore. The attention goes to the picture that is formed.

Let's look now at three lessons we can learn from the illustration of the puzzle.

> What are your strengths? Weaknesses? What do you need from fellow Christians? What can you offer them?
>
> _____
>
> _____
>
> _____

Even Seemingly Insignificant Parts Are Important

I used to be fascinated by a passage in Judges 1:1-7 where Judah and Simeon captured a Canaanite king named Adoni-Bezek, and, giving him a taste of his own medicine, cut off his thumbs and big toes. (Adoni-Bezek, you see, had done this same thing to 70 kings *he* had captured!) I never fully understood the purpose, I guess, until someone explained to me that both grip and balance are greatly affected by the loss of seemingly insignificant digits.

Back in March of 1981, Ronald Reagan, then President of the United States, was shot by John Hinckley, Jr. As he recovered from his injuries, Reagan was hospitalized for a period of several weeks. Although he was our nation's chief executive at the time, his convalescence had surprisingly little impact on the government's activity. Business proceeded pretty much as usual. At nearly the same time, however, in the city of Philadelphia, Pennsylvania, some garbage collectors went on strike, and chaos erupted in a relatively short period of time. Not only was the city literally a mess, but piles of decaying trash became a serious health concern.

Now if I were to ask you, "Who do you think has the most important job: a garbage man or the President of the United States?" How would you respond? I know what my reply would be, without hesitation! But actually, when you think about it, whose absence was felt the most?

There are a lot of people in our congregations with "garbage man" roles. In other words, they are behind-the-scenes workers, doing tasks that often go unnoticed and unappreciated. They are not the leaders we see standing before us in public assemblies; they may

> *Who has the most important job — a garbage man or the President?*

not even be the ones who get mentioned in the bulletin. But just like thumbs and big toes, they have a place, an *important* place in the body.

Name some people who fill "garbage man" roles in your congregation. How can you show them your appreciation?

_____

_____

_____

No One Part Should Dominate or Feel Superior

Everyone has a place in the body of Christ, and everyone should remember his or her place. This point can be illustrated by an incident from the life of the French sculptor Francois Rodin.

According to all accounts, Rodin once spent a lengthy period of time working on a statue designed to pay homage to the writer Honore de Balzac. When he at last finished the piece, it was four o'clock in the morning. Eager to get someone's reaction to his work, he awakened one of the art students who was staying there at his studio. The student stumbled in and sleepily surveyed the figure of Balzac. In the statue, Balzac was wearing a long, flowing robe with loose sleeves and had his hands folded in the front. "Wonderful!" the student exclaimed giddily. "What hands! I have never in my life seen such marvelous hands!"

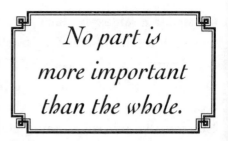

No part is more important than the whole.

Rodin's face supposedly darkened. Without saying a word, he went and awakened another young artist, but the reaction he received was the same. A third student, too, seemed overpowered by the beauty of this one particular feature.

At that point, something in Rodin seemed to snap. With a cry, he rushed over to a corner of the studio and pulled out an axe. His students tried to restrain him, but he pushed them aside and with one quick blow, chopped off the statue's hands. "I was forced to destroy them," he later explained, "because they had a life of their own. They did not belong to the rest of the composition."

"Remember this, and remember it well," he advised his students, when discussing the incident afterwards. *"No part is more important than the whole."*

Today in Paris, the statue of Balzac stands, without hands, for all to see. Many assume the hands are merely covered by the large robe sleeves, but in reality Rodin broke them off in an effort to preserve unity in his masterpiece.

> Who are some individuals you can think of in the Bible who struggled at times with trying to dominate or feeling superior to others?
>
> _____
>
> _____
>
> _____

ALL PARTS ARE CONNECTED

When our youngest daughter, Bethany, was two, she got a finger closed in the bathroom door at a fast food restaurant and nearly lost the end of her pinky. Until it began to heal properly, we were told to keep the wound bandaged. Every day, we had to remove the wrapping and clean the reattached fingertip. Because I am weak-stomached (and a coward at heart!), I took her over to a neighbor of my mom's, who just happened to be a registered nurse, and got her to do it for me. I remember one day, standing there in the kitchen, watching my baby as Janie carefully removed the gauze. Bethany was biting her little lip, trying so hard to be brave. As the bandage was being gently pulled away from the finger on her left hand, I looked, and guess what the little finger on her *right hand* was doing? It was perpendicular to the other fingers—stiff, tense, and taut. The reason? It was feeling the pain for that other little pinky! And why was that, do you think? Because those two fingers are connected. They are part of the same body.

> *When one of us hurts, we should all hurt. When one of us rejoices, we should all rejoice.*

In the church, we are also connected to one another. So when one of us hurts, we should all hurt. When one of us re- joices, we should all rejoice (Romans 12:15). That is what being a body is all about.

I love the story Lyn Rose tells in the book *Mom's Diary* about the little girl who came home late from a friend's house. When her mother questioned her about the tardiness, the little girl explained that her friend's doll broke. "So did you stay to help her fix it?" the mother asked. "No," the little girl replied, "I stayed to help her cry." We all have times when we need someone to help us cry, just as there are times we need someone to help us rejoice, and times when we need someone just to help us *period*. No one can fill these roles any better than a brother or sister in Christ.

Has there ever been an occasion in your life when someone "helped" you cry? When and why? What did that kind of comfort mean to you?

_____

_____

_____

SUGGESTIONS FOR CLOSER FELLOWSHIP

(1) We need to know each other more than just superficially. When my husband and I worked with young people, I once hosted a makeover party for the teenage girls. Upon her arrival, the first thing our Mary Kay representative did was ask the girls to remove all their makeup. Without a second's hesitation, they complied. (And why not? Most 15- and 16-year-olds are just as pretty—or prettier!—without makeup as they are with it.) I feel sure, however, that a group of my peers would not have been nearly as eager to oblige. You see, we are much better (much more experienced, I suppose) at *concealing* our flaws than we are at revealing them.

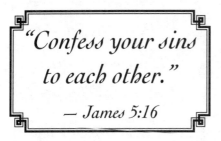

"Confess your sins to each other."

— *James 5:16*

I ran into an acquaintance early one morning at the grocery store. She apparently had rushed in hurriedly, just for a couple of items, and blushingly confided that I had caught her without her makeup. I understood her embarrassment; the same thing has happened to me (and probably to most women) at one time or another. It makes us uncomfortable when people see us as we really are physically, flaws and all. Unfortunately, the same thing is often true spiritually. We want to present an impressive, "I've-got-it-all-together" look, whether or not that is accurate. How much better off we would be if we could just be honest with one another. Surely this was God's intent when He inspired James to write, "confess your sins to each other" (James 5:16).

(2) We need to accept one another. Surveys have shown that "being accepted" is what young people desire above all else. I am not sure we adults are a lot different. Why does a man go into his neighborhood bar

How important is it for the body of Christ to be accepting of others? Who were some "outcasts" Jesus accepted?

_____

_____

_____

every day after work? Perhaps because that is where he feels accepted. Remember that old theme song from the television sitcom *Cheers*?

> Sometimes you want to go
> Where everybody knows your name
> And they're always glad you came.
> You want to be where you can see
> Troubles are all the same
> You want to go
> Where everybody knows your name.

At the end of the Korean War, a mother received a phone call from her son in the service. "I'm in San Diego," the son said, "and I'm coming home." Needless to say, the mother was overjoyed to learn that her son was alive. "There's just one thing, Mom," he said. "I'm bringing a buddy with me who got hurt pretty bad. He only has one eye, one arm and one leg. He has no home, and I want him to live with us."

"Well, sure," the mom replied. "He can stay for a while."

"No, you don't understand," the son said. "I want him to be with us always. He's in bad shape."

Somewhat impatient, the mom said, "Son, you're too emotional about this. You've been in the war. Don't you see that this buddy of yours will only drag you down?"

Without discussing it further, the two said their goodbyes and hung up. The next day, the mother received a shocking telegram from the Navy, informing her that her son had leaped to his death from the twelfth floor of a San Diego hotel. A few days later, when his body was shipped home, it turned out that *he* was the soldier with one eye, one arm and one leg. He did not have the courage to come home because he didn't think he would be accepted as he was.

As Christians, we all have battle wounds. We also have idiosyncrasies, faults, and annoying habits. Jesus, however, has accepted us with open—and forgiving—arms. Now if only we, His followers, could be that accepting!

(3) *We need to support one another.* In my book, *Playing the Hand You Are Dealt*, Nina Hargett related the value of a support group as she struggled to deal with the death of her son Robert. In today's society, there are

support groups for everything. (I even heard about one for adults whose mothers had thrown away their baseball cards!) Such groups are effective because of the close affinity that exists among those who have shared a common experience. (And isn't it this very thing that makes Jesus such a suitable mediator for us? Hebrews 4:15 says, "For we do not have a high priest who is unable to sympathize with our weaknesses, but we have one who has been tempted in every way, just as we are. . . . ")

If I am facing the challenge of raising toddlers, how reassuring it is to be able to talk to an older mom who has been there (and survived it!). The same goes for the hectic and harried teenage years. God knew how valuable such support would be (Titus 2:3-5).

> *"For we do not have a high priest who is unable to sympathize with our weaknesses . . ."*
>
> — *Hebrews 4:15*

(4) *We need to cheer each other on.* In *Wind and Fire*, Bruce Larson lists three remarkable qualities of Sandhill Cranes, large birds that fly great distances across continents. First, they rotate leadership (in other words, no one bird stays out front all the time). Second, they choose leaders who can handle turbulence. Third, during the time one bird is leading, the others are busy honking their affirmation. We do a lot of honking in the church, but I am not sure it is honking of affirmation! Yet this is what we so desperately need. We need to be like Aaron and Hur in Exodus 17:8-13 who held up Moses' hands until the battle was won.

(5) *We need to realize the importance of being together.* An incident that took place once in Point Barrow, Alaska illustrates this so well. Somehow, three gray whales had come too far inland and were gasping for breath around a hole in the ice. The only hope for their survival was to transport them five miles past the ice strip back out to the open sea. Rescuers began cutting a string of "breathing holes" about twenty yards apart in the six-inch thick ice. For eight days, they coaxed the whales from one hole to the next, mile after mile. Along the way, one of the whales vanished, but the other two were eventually able to swim to freedom.

For Christians, our times together are "breathing holes." Just like those whales, you see, we swim in murky waters every day, fighting for survival. But when we meet for worship and fellowship, it is like coming to the surface and filling our lungs once more with air. Those moments are the only thing that keep us going. They enable us to dive back down once again, swim a little further, and travel closer on toward our ultimate destination.

Has there ever been a time in your life when (due to illness, perhaps) you were unable to attend worship services on a regular basis? What did you miss? Was your spiritual life affected?

_____

_____

_____

SUMMARY

One of the added benefits of walking in the light is the fellowship we have one with another. This fellowship not only draws believers together, it strengthens and solidifies us as well. We are capable of much more as a unit than we are as individuals. With a common goal, we can thus help one another along the journey.

CHAPTER 9

Staying in the Circle:

Continual Cleansing

I do a lot of laundry. At least I did when all four of our children still lived at home. During the years when they were teenagers and all played on sports teams, it seemed my washing machine was in constant use. I used to joke that our clothes hamper was like the widow's bin in 1 Kings 17. Remember that story? The widow of Zarephath baked bread, baked bread, and baked bread, but never ran out of flour. In a similar way, I did laundry, did laundry, and did laundry, but never ran out of clothes to wash!

Mothers of large families are not the only ones with this kind of challenge. In a spiritual sense, we all are in need of cleansing. Continually.

> *"If we walk in the light . . . the blood of Jesus . . . purifies us from all sin."*
> — 1 John 1:7

Fortunately, the blood of Jesus is well-equipped for the task. 1 John 1:7 offers this assurance: "if we walk in the light as He is in the light . . . the blood of Jesus, His Son, cleanses us from all sin." (NKJV) Greek scholars are quick to point out that the beauty in this concept springs from a point of grammar. The verb tense, you see, indicates that the action is *continual*.

OUR SIN PROBLEM

Romans 3:23 states something that comes as no surprise to any of us. According to Paul, "all have sinned and fall short of the glory of God." The persecutor-turned-apostle certainly knew what he was talking about; in 1 Timothy 1:15 he said, "Christ Jesus came into the world to save sinners—of whom I am the worst." While Paul may have been the worst, he definitely was not the first. Adam and Eve have that distinction. They "missed the mark"—sin's literal definition—back in the garden, in the very beginning of time. And though we, their descendants, did not inherit the sin, we did inherit their self-seeking tendencies. Unfortunately, those tendencies have been getting us into trouble ever since.

Just what has come about as a result of all this sin? Isaiah describes it this way: "But your iniquities have separated you from your God; your sins have hidden his face from you, so that he will not hear" (Isaiah 59:2).

God, you see, is holy and pure. Unlike His human offspring, there is no sin in Him. In fact, it is contrary to His very nature.

When I was young, I heard an illustration concerning God's righteousness that was so apt I have never forgotten it.

Let's just suppose that you have a pet dog you keep inside your home. You have had him ever since

> *"Your iniquities have separated you from your God; your sins have hidden his face from you."*
> — *Isaiah 59:2*

he was just a puppy, and you love that dog immensely. He pretty much has the run of the house, curling up on the sofa by you when you are watching television, even sleeping at the foot of your bed.

One day, however, when you come home, you find that your dog has gotten out and wandered over to an empty lot next door where construction has begun for a new house. It has been raining all day and the building site is a mess. So is your dog. He is covered with mud from head to toe. But upon your arrival, he comes bounding over to you as if nothing has happened. He is ready to jump into your arms and have you pet him.

What is your reaction? Do you still love your dog? Of course you do. But in his present state, can you welcome him into your presence? Absolutely not. Not until he is clean.

Simplistic though it may be, that scenario is very similar to a sinner's attempt to approach God. Does God love us despite our erring ways? You bet He does. But can He welcome us in our sinful state into His presence? No. At least not until we have been cleansed.

Contrast the difference in our nature with the nature of God.

_____

_____

_____

_____

POWER IN THE BLOOD

With our defilement due to sin so evident, it is reassuring to know that a solution exists. Isaiah 1:18 says, "Though your sins are like scarlet, they shall be as white as snow; though they are red as crimson, they shall be like wool." But just exactly how does this purification come about?

Revelation 1:5 tells us that Jesus Christ "loved us and washed us from our sins in his own blood (NKJV)."

To those of us in modern times who tend to think of blood more as something that *causes* stains rather than re-

> *"Blood . . . makes atonement for one's life."*
> — *Leviticus 17:11*

moves them, this idea seems almost contradictory. But to those with a background in the old law, the concept was easily understood. Blood as a cleansing agent was a no-brainer to them. According to Leviticus 17:11, "it is . . . blood that makes atonement for one's life." And "without the shedding of blood there is no forgiveness" (Hebrews 9:22).

In the Old Testament, of course, the bloodshed involved animal sacrifices. But the sacrifice for our sins was Jesus Himself. Here is just a sampling of what scripture has to say about the power in His blood:

"For if the blood of bulls and goats and the ashes of a heifer, sprinkling the unclean, sanctifies for the purifying of the flesh, how much more shall the blood of Christ , who through the eternal Spirit offered Himself without spot to God, cleanse your conscience from good works to serve a living God?" (Hebrews 9:13,14 NKJV).

"Since we have now been justified by his blood, how much more shall we be saved from God's wrath through Him" (Romans 5:9).

"In him we have redemption through his blood, the forgiveness of sins, in accordance with the riches of God's grace" (Ephesians 1:7).

"But now in Christ Jesus, you who once were far away have been brought near through the blood of Christ" (Ephesians 2:13).

"[W]e have redemption through his blood, the forgiveness of sins" (Colossians 1:14, NKJV).

"[T]hey have washed their robes and made them white in the blood of the Lamb" (Revelation 7:14).

In her book *Really Bad Girls of the Bible*, Liz Curtis Higgs draws a comparison between Jesus' blood and the woman with the issue of blood in Luke 8:

> Consider this: The Lord stopped her flow of
> blood even as he prepared to shed his own blood
> that the whole world might live. As women who
> understand all too well what it means to bleed,
> we are grateful that her endless flow ceased.
> But we're exceedingly more grateful that the
> blood of Jesus has not stopped flowing for
> two thousand years. It is in his blood that we
> find our freedom!

What significance does the blood of Christ have to you? What difference has it made in your life?

_____

_____

_____

"YOU CAN'T CLEAN THEM YOURSELF"

I love the story Zig Ziglar tells about stuffing some really dirty clothes soiled from yard work in the trunk of his car, then promptly forgetting about them. Several days later, upon discovering them, he carried the smelly bundle into the cleaners. Embarrassed at the condition of the garments, he apologized repeatedly. "They're such a mess, I was almost ashamed to bring them in," he said.

The attendant smiled. "The only reason we're here," he said, "is to clean up your dirty clothes. We're glad they're in a mess! We're glad you can't clean them

> *If we could clean up the mess we make of our lives, there would be no need for Calvary.*

yourself, because if you could, there would be no reason for our being here."

If we could clean up the mess we make of our lives, Ziglar says, there would be no need for Calvary. But as we all know, we cannot. We are stained with sin and helpless to do anything about it. Fortunately for us, that is where our Savior comes in.

THE GIFT THAT KEEPS ON GIVING

Jesus' blood was shed in His death on the cross. Romans 6:4 tells us that in baptism we are buried into His death. The water is where we come in contact with His blood.

But just because I have come in contact with the blood, just because I have been saved through baptism (1 Peter 3:21), just because I am now in Christ (2 Corinthians 5:17) and walking in the light, that does not mean that I will not ever sin anymore. Romans 8:1 does not say that there is no more sin for those who are in Christ Jesus. It says there is no more *condemnation* for sin.

Even as a Christian, I am going to mess up, and mess up plenty. But just as sin tries to regain its hold on me, Christ's blood continues to wipe it away.

> *Romans 8:1 doesn't say there is no more sin. It says there is no more condemnation for sin.*

Compare it to a "continual cleaning" oven (was not *that* a great invention?). Remember in older models where the residue would build up over a period of time until cleaning became a major undertaking? With "continual cleaning," that no longer happens. In a similar way, God does not let sin "build up" in the life of a Christian. As long as we are in fellowship with Him, He is going to cleanse it as it occurs. We are not going to be controlled by it as we once may have been.

Another example we might look to is that of windshield wipers. As rain falls, a car's wipers—when engaged—continually remove the drops from a driver's field of vision. It is an ongoing process, and an essential one in a rainstorm. As Christians, we need God's windshield wipers to remove the sin in our life. As long as we "engage them," by walking in the light, He promises us that the cleansing is going to take place.

A third illustration we might use is our computers. Most all of us, I imagine, use these wonderful inventions either at home or in our work. I still know very little about the technical aspects of computers, however, and at times am made to feel very foolish where they are concerned.

I read a story about a woman named Judy, editor of a trivia publication, who was having trouble with her computer. So she called Dave, a computer expert, over to her desk. He clicked a couple of buttons on the keyboard and, in no time at all, solved her problem.

As he was walking away, Judy called after him, "Well, what was wrong, anyway?"

He shrugged. "It was just an ID ten T error," he replied.

A puzzled expression came over Judy's face. "An ID ten T error? What's that. . . in case I need to fix it again?"

He grinned. "Haven't you heard of an ID ten T error before?" he asked.

"No," she replied.

"Write it down," he said, "and I think you'll figure it out."

So she did. She wrote: ID10T.

I can sympathize with Judy. There is so little I really understand about computers that at times I truly feel like an idiot.

And that is how it is with living the Christian life. We make dumb mistakes; we flub up again and again. There is so much to learn and so little we truly understand.

But isn't it great to have an expert we can call on, someone who is always willing to help? God comes to our aid time and time again. He never criticizes or laughs at us. He just "re-boots us," if you will, and gets us back on track once more.

What are some problems you seem to battle continually? How does it make you feel to know that God doesn't give up on you?

_____

_____

_____

_____

FIT FOR HIS PRESENCE

There is one other aspect of this cleaning process that we would do well to consider.

In 1 John 1:7, the Greek word used for "cleanses" originally described ceremonial washings that qualified a man to approach his gods. These were elaborate procedures in the eastern culture. (Back in Exodus 19, we see something very similar when the children of Israel spent three days preparing themselves to go before God.)

But as religion developed, the term came to have more of a moral sense and described a goodness that enabled a man to enter God's fellowship. Of course, we know that on our own, without Christ, we would never be good enough to enter God's presence.

When I think of what Christ has done for us, I am reminded of a passage in Isaiah 61:10: "For he has clothed me with garments of salvation and arrayed me in a robe of righteousness...." This verse was brought to life for me in a very real way a few years ago when my husband and I went to see our daughter perform in a band concert at her school. We had arrived early, and I was standing in the foyer of the auditorium,

> *"He has clothed me with garments of salvation and arrayed me in a robe of righteousness."*
>
> — *Isaiah 61:10*

talking to a friend, when her husband came walking up to join us. My friend gave her husband a rather strange look and asked, "Where on earth did you get that shirt?" He didn't reply, just stood there grinning as she exclaimed, "That's not the shirt you were wearing when we left our house a few minutes ago! You don't even own a shirt like that!"

Her husband proceeded to explain that, after letting her out at the door, he was driving around in search of a parking place when he saw one of the band members out in front of the gym. For some reason, that particular young man did not know, did not understand, or simply did not follow the instructions to wear a white dress shirt for the performance. Instead he had worn a very bright, loud plaid shirt. His shirt, however, was not acceptable to the band director, and therefore he was not going to be allowed to be a part of the afternoon performance.

Thanks to my friend's husband, though, he made it on stage after all. How was it possible? This compassionate man took off his own white dress shirt and gave it to the young musician. (It did not really fit, of course, but that hardly mattered.) Then he took the smaller loud plaid shirt and squeezed himself into it.

That is exactly what Jesus did for us! Isaiah 64:6 says our own personal righteousness is like "filthy rags." But Jesus took that on Himself and gave us His righteousness. When He lived here on this earth, you see, He completely obeyed God's laws. He never once sinned. That spotless record of His becomes ours. So now, when God looks at us, He doesn't see filthy rags anymore. He sees a clean white dress shirt, the one Jesus placed on us.

Remember back in the Garden of Eden when God made clothes for Adam and Eve to cover their nakedness? I have always thought of that as such a special gesture. With loving hands, from animal skins, He formed clothing to drape on them. Centuries later, He has done the same thing for His children. He has covered us with righteousness!

Write a prayer, thanking Jesus for what He has done.

A PROCESS OF CHANGING

Once we accept Christ's sacrifice on our behalf, we begin a process of trying to become more like Him. We long for the righteousness with which we have been credited. As a result, we strive daily to add loveliness and holiness to our lives. Sure, we understand that no matter what we do, we will never be worthy on our own merits. But out of gratitude for the cleansing that has taken place, we "are being transformed into his likeness" (2 Corinthians 3:18).

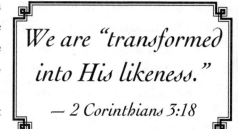

We are "transformed into His likeness."

— 2 Corinthians 3:18

Has anyone ever told you that you look more like your mother every day? Oh, what a wonderful compliment for Christians if we could be told, "You are more like your Father every day!"

I read a story once about a preacher who, like most ministers, went to visit new parents after their first baby was born. He said without fail, the fathers would always say (especially if the child were a boy), "Don't you think he looks like me?"

"I never saw a baby who looked like *anybody*," the preacher thought. "Babies look like babies!" But of course he kept these opinions to himself.

A year or so later, the preacher would go and visit the family again, and again he would hear the same question. He had to admit the baby did not look like it had twelve months earlier, but he still kept his thoughts to himself: *A chubby little fellow with a saggy diaper and a runny nose? He didn't look much like anybody yet.*

At five years of age, the father would ask the same question. "Don't you think he looks like me?" The preacher might admit, "Well, maybe a little bit, but not much."

However, by the time the boy reached fifteen, something strange had taken place. He *had* begun to look like him. And at 21, the resemblance was undeniable. The older he got, the more obvious it became. He was the spitting image of his father.

So it is with the Christian life. When we first became a Christian, we did not look much like God. But as the years go by, as we are continually cleansed and continually growing, we come to resemble our Father more and more.

> Which relative in your family do you favor the most physically? What are some characteristics you think you inherited from your ancestors? Which of God's qualities do you find the hardest to emulate? Easiest?
>
> _____
> _____
> _____
> _____
> _____
> _____
> _____
> _____

Summary

Man has a sin problem. Defiled and contaminated because of his evil ways, he can no longer have fellowship with a pure and holy God.

The situation is rectified, however, by the cleansing blood of Jesus Christ. On the cross, Jesus took on our sins and gave us His righteousness.

By coming in contact with His blood through baptism, our guilt can be removed. Then, as we walk in the light, His blood continues to keep us clean.

CHAPTER 10

Staying in the Circle:

Safety and Protection

My husband and I have three little nieces who live in California. We do not see them (or their parents, for that matter) nearly as often as we'd like.

Whenever we are together, though, we enjoy a running gag that has become somewhat of a tradition. No one can remember just how it started, but it entails Uncle Roger threatening to "eat" (i.e., tickle) the little girls' toes. Oh, how they squeal and giggle, as they jump out of his reach, run to the sofa, and tuck their feet under themselves. It has really become a game; one they love dearly. Even when we talk on the phone, they courageously insist that, next visit, they are not going to let him eat their toes. (Of course, they would be disappointed if he didn't even try!)

When Emily, the youngest, was new to the routine, she thought she had found a solution. While big sisters Katie and Melinda scampered away to safety, she firmly stood her ground. "Uncle Roger's gonna get your toes!" her siblings, huddled on the couch, warned.

"He can't," was her reply. "I've got socks on!"

Emily's security, stemming from the fact that her toes were covered, pinpoints yet another benefit that comes from our walking in the light.

> "He is my refuge and my fortress, my God, in whom I trust."
> — Psalm 91:2

Within the circle of God's communion, obedient to His will, we not only have fellowship and continual cleansing. We have safety and protection as well.

"He who dwells in the shelter of the Most High will rest in the shadow of the Almighty. I will say of the Lord, "He is my refuge and my fortress, my God in whom I trust. He will cover you. . . " (Psalm 91:1-2, 4).

A MOTHER'S LOVE

We all know there are many places in the Bible where God is compared to a loving father, not the least of which is the story of the Prodigal Son in Luke 15. But did you know there is also a passage that compares Him to a mother? In Deuteronomy 33:12, in a blessing on Benjamin,

Moses wrote, "The beloved of the Lord shall dwell in safety by him; and the Lord shall cover him all the day long, and he shall dwell between his shoulders" (KJV).

In the Far East, in Bible times, tent and village mothers not only cared for their households, they also went out to work in the fields. Their babies were taken along with them, like a papoose, in camel's hair cradles they carried on their backs. As the mother labored, the baby would sleep in safety between her shoulders. When the sun grew warmer, the mother carefully covered her child with her large white veil, protecting it from the heat and insects.

God offers His children a similar safety. Amid the cares of life, we can be assured that He looks out for our needs. "Rest in the Lord, and wait patiently for Him; do not fret. . . " (Psalm 37:7, NKJV).

> *"Rest in the Lord, and wait patiently for Him; do not fret."*
> — *Psalm 37:7, NKJV*

In *Chicken Soup for the Mother's Soul*, Jim Stovall elaborates on the type of protection a mother provides in a piece entitled "Moving Mountains."

> There were two warring tribes in the Andes, one that lived in the lowlands and the other high in the mountains. The mountain people invaded the lowlanders one day, and as part of their plundering of the people, they kidnapped a baby of one of the lowlander families and took the infant with them back up into the mountains.
>
> The lowlanders didn't know how to climb the mountain. They didn't know any of the trails that the mountain people used, and they didn't know where to find the mountain people or how to track them in the steep terrain.
>
> Even so, they sent out their best party of fighting men to climb the mountain and bring the baby home.
>
> The men tried first one method of climbing and then another. They tried one trail and then another. After several days of effort, however, they had climbed only a couple of hundred feet.

Feeling hopeless and helpless, the lowlander men decided that the cause was lost, and they prepared to return to the village below.

As they were packing their gear for the descent, they saw the baby's mother walking toward them. They realized that she was coming down the mountain that they hadn't figured out how to climb.

And then they saw that she had the baby strapped to her back. *How could that be?*

One man greeted her and said, "We couldn't climb this mountain. How did you do this when we, the strongest and most able men in the village, couldn't do it?"

She shrugged her shoulders and said, "It wasn't your baby."

Just as a mother would do anything for her child, God has done everything for us. "How great is the love the Father has lavished on us, that we should be called children of God! And that is what we are!" (I John 3:1).

> Think of instances you know about personally or have heard in the news where mothers did extraordinary things for their children.
>
> _____
>
> _____
>
> _____
>
> _____

A SHEPHERD'S CARE

Another image that scripture uses to convey God's role as a protector is that of a shepherd. I love Isaiah's description of the security He provides: "He shall feed his flock like a shepherd: he shall gather the lambs with his arm, and carry them in his bosom, and shall gently lead those that are with young" (Isaiah 40:11, KJV).

The Bible, we know, was written—through the guidance of the Holy Spirit, of course—by very simple, average men. Not only was it written by common men, it was written *for* the common man, an audience of country-dwellers, all well-acquainted with the ways of nature. Unfortunately, today most of us who read and study God's Word live

> *"He shall gather the lambs with his arm, and carry them in his bosom . . ."*
> —*Isaiah 40:11*

in cities and are not very familiar with subjects such as livestock or crops. (An incident that occurred several years ago illustrates just how much things have changed. My second son, Luke, three at the time, was asked in Bible class where we get our milk. Instead of the expected reply—*from cows*—he animatedly responded, "From the store!") Even those of us today who might tend a vegetable garden or even own some cattle probably still know very little about sheep.

I certainly didn't. When one of my girls was in grade school, I went on a field trip with her class to a sheep farm, and was shocked at what I saw. These were not the beautiful, soft, little white creatures I had seen in storybooks next to Little Bo Peep! I was very disillusioned. These sheep were dirty, their wool was matted, and the sound they made was quite irritating.

Our guide that day informed us that sheep are weak, dumb, nearsighted, prone to drowning, and have no sense of direction whatsoever. "Wow!" I thought to myself. "That reminds me of *me*."

Like sheep, I am in need of someone to watch after me. Who better to do that than the One who made me?

Read Psalm 23. Which verses give you the most comfort and delight? Why?

_____

_____

_____

_____

_____

"The Lord Is My Shepherd"

Probably the best-known and most quoted scripture in the Bible is Psalm 23, a detailed depiction of God in His Shepherd's role. Let's look at a few of the key phrases.

David begins the passage by using a personal pronoun: "The Lord is *my* shepherd." In other words, we belong to Him.

> *Oh, what special treatment we receive from the Lord!*

When our family lived in Brazil, there was a girl who came to our home and worked a couple of days each week. (Granted, at first I felt almost guilty employing household help. But considering some of my circumstances—no hot water, no glass in my windows, lizards on the ceiling, and four young children underfoot—I quickly got over it and learned to appreciate a culture where that was the norm!) Teresa had no husband, three children of her own, and a very hard life. We tried to help her as best we could, and I often gave her things my own children had outgrown. Sometimes she would come to me and ask about a particular item she had spotted: a pair of shoes—old, scuffed up, almost too small. "Sure," I'd say. "Go on. Take them."

Given my consent, Teresa proceeded to spend what seemed like hours working on those shoes—cleaning, polishing, making them look so good that I was tempted to change my mind and keep them! (I wanted to say, "Why didn't you do that before?") The difference, of course, was that now *they belonged to her*. Oh, what special treatment we receive from the Lord! What good care He takes of us. We belong to Him, we are His.

"I Shall Not Want"

When we think of not wanting anything, we may imagine Ed McMahon showing up on our doorstep with a giant check from Publisher's Clearinghouse, or a genie who emerges from a bottle to grant our every wish. But the word "want" used in Psalm 23:1 (KJV) has a much broader meaning. Although it implies we will not lack for anything (and Matthew 6:25-33 assures this), it also includes the idea of being utterly contented in the Good Shepherd's care. This, of course, is reminiscent of Paul's statement in Philippians 4:11, "I have learned to be content whatever the circumstances."

As part of God's flock, I should be completely satisfied with His management of my life. I should accept the fact that He is in control.

> *"I have learned to be content whatever the circumstances."*
> —*Philippians 4:11*

Now, granted, that is not always easy to do. Like Abraham and Sarah, we often feel like we need to help God out, especially when things are not moving along as quickly as we would like (see Genesis 16).

Once in a mechanic's shop, I saw a sign that expressed the following sentiment:

LABOR RATES

Normal	$12.50 per hour
If you wait	$15.00 per hour
If you watch	$20.00 per hour
If you help	$30.00 per hour
If you laugh	$40.00 per hour
If you worked on it first	$70.00 per hour

"HE LEADETH ME BESIDE THE STILL WATERS"

Although sheep thrive in dry, semi-arid country, they still require water. But, because they are easily spooked, they will not drink from moving streams. In his book, *A Shepherd Looks at Psalm 23*, Phillip Keller provides additional insight. According to him, sheep can go for months on end, provided the weather is not too hot, without actually drinking—if there is heavy dew on the grass each morning. By habit, sheep rise early, just before dawn, and begin to feed. The early hours are when the vegetation is drenched with dew, and sheep can keep fit on the amount of water taken in with their forage when they graze just before and after dawn.

Even so, in the Christian life, those who are often the most serene and most secure in the midst of all of life's challenges are those who rise early each day to feed on God's Word. Now I must admit that this is something I have always seemed to struggle with doing on a regular basis. I usually stay up late, and as a result have a hard time parting with my pillow in the morning. But we know that while here on the earth, Jesus consistently exhibited this type of discipline. "Very early in the morning, while it was still dark, Jesus got up, left the house and went off to a solitary place, where he prayed" (Mark 1:35).

Certainly we will be more aware of God's guidance and protection in our busy lives when we start the day by spending time with Him.

> I got up early one morning
> And rushed right into the day;
> I had so much to accomplish
> That I didn't have time to pray.
>
> Problems just tumbled about me,
> And heavier came each task.
> "Why doesn't God help me?" I wondered.
> He answered, "You didn't ask."
>
> I wanted to see joy and beauty,
> But the day toiled on, gray and bleak;
> I wondered why God didn't show me.
> He said, "But you didn't seek."
>
> I tried to come into God's presence;
> I used all my keys at the lock.
> God gently and lovingly chided,
> "My child, you didn't knock."
>
> I woke up early this morning,
> And paused before entering the day;
> I had so much to accomplish
> That I had to take time to pray.

What are some benefits of spending time at the start of the day with God? What are some things you can change about your personal routine in order to make it possible for you to do this?

_____

_____

_____

"HE RESTORETH MY SOUL"

Does your soul ever need restoring? Do you ever feel cast down? David, the author of Psalm 23, experienced this; in Psalm 42:11 he wrote, "Why are you downcast, O my soul?"

Interestingly enough, there is a parallel to this same type of circumstance with sheep. "Being cast" is an old English shepherd's term for what happens when a sheep is turned over on his back and cannot get up on his own. (Much like the June bugs we would play with when I was a kid—this is the image that keeps popping into my mind!) Shepherds keep a close watch out for sheep that are cast. If they do not arrive on the scene within a reasonable period of time, the sheep will die or else be eaten by a predator.

Which sheep do you think are the most susceptible to being cast? They are the fat sheep, the sheep that have too much wool, the sheep that choose to lie down in soft, comfortable, rounded hollows in the ground.

In the Christian life, there is also a danger in becoming too comfortable.

> *"Woe to them that are at ease in Zion."*
> — *Amos 6:1, KJV*

I am reminded of a phrase I used to hear said that the purpose of the Bible is two-fold: to comfort the afflicted, and to afflict the comfortable! Amos 6:1 warns, "Woe to them that are at ease in Zion" (KJV). The New International Version puts it this way: "Woe to you who are complacent. . . ."

"I WILL DWELL IN THE HOUSE OF THE LORD FOREVER"

A consignment of sheep had been sent from Scotland to Australia. Along with them had been sent a generous supply of hay, enough to last the entire journey. Just before reaching the destination, however, the sheep suddenly refused to eat. At the same time, a dense fog covered the waters. For two days, the ship was obliged to stop. The sheep still would not eat, and their owner was becoming quite worried. When the fog lifted, however, he could see before him the green fields of Australia and realized what had happened. The sheep had smelled the fresh pasture land ahead, not too far in the distance, and had lost their appetite for dried hay.

The closer we get to our heavenly home, the less appetite we should have for the things of this world. We should cling even more closely to our wonderful Shepherd, lovingly accept His guidance and protection, and let Him safely lead us home.

> In what ways does your attitude about physical things change as you mature? Your attitude about spiritual things?
>
> _____
>
> _____
>
> _____
>
> _____

SUMMARY

God has covered us, not only with His love, but with His protection as well. According to Psalm 91:4, under His wings we have refuge.

This security He provides is not unlike the well-being a selfless mother makes possible for her child. The Bible also compares it to the shepherd's care for his flock.

CHAPTER 11

Stained Glass Saints: Biblical Examples

As a young boy and his mother toured one of the great cathedrals in southern France, the youngster was enthralled by the church's beautiful stained glass windows. He paused and carefully examined each one. Delighted over his curiosity, the mother used the opportunity to

> *Throughout the Bible, we have numerous examples of individuals through whom the light of God shines.*

relate to the boy life stories of each of the Biblical characters depicted.

Upon returning to their hotel, the lad was met by his grandmother who had stayed behind. "Well," she asked eagerly, "what did you think of the cathedral?"

"Oh, Grandma," he replied. "It was beautiful! I saw all the different saints!"

"You did?" she said. "And exactly whom do you consider a saint?"

"You know, Grandma," the boy responded. "They're those people the light shines through!"

Throughout the Bible, we have numerous examples of individuals through whom the light of God shines very plainly.

In this chapter, we will look at two of them.

A LIGHT GIVER

Several years ago on Wednesday nights, I taught a ladies' class entitled *Little Known Women of the Bible*. One of my favorite lessons in that series came from Judges 4 and 5 and centered around a fascinating woman whose name was Deborah.

Historical accounts from that period say that Deborah may have once been a keeper of the tabernacle lamps. If this is true, it is consistent with the fact that God often chose people from very humble and simple walks of life to

> *Deborah may have been a keeper of the tabernacle lamps.*

do some of His greatest tasks. (In fact, in the very next chapter, Judges 6, Gideon tries to avoid the Lord's call by saying in verse 15, "My clan is the weakest in Manasseh, and I am the least in my family.") Deborah's tabernacle duty as a light keeper would also be symbolic of her later years when she gave light to all of Israel in quite a different way.

FIRST AND FOREMOST, A MOM

If one were to write a resume for Deborah, numerous positions could be listed. At various stages of her life, she was a counselor, a prophetess, a poet, a singer, and a judge (holding court—of all places!—under a palm tree), not to mention a leader in war. Talk about multi-tasking.

Deborah lived some thirteen centuries before Christ, and, as far as we know, she is the only woman in the Bible placed at the pinnacle of the political power in her day by the consent of the people.

What strikes me most about her, though, is the fact that she never seemed to seek—or, for that matter, even desire—the position. Look at the way she described herself in Judges 5:7. In the victory song, after the children of Israel had defeated their enemy, what did she say? She did not say, "I, Deborah, the judge," nor "I, Deborah, the prophetess," nor "I, Deborah, the military leader." Rather she said, "I, Deborah, a *mother in Israel.*" That shows a tremendous amount of humility. But even more, I think it indicates that of all the things she did, she felt her role in the home was the most important.

> *Of all the things she did, she felt her role in the home was the most important.*

Some who look at Deborah say, "Ah, here was the first great feminist!" or "This story proves (a la Annie Oakley) that anything men can do, women can do better." But I think people of such opinions miss the point entirely. Many of Deborah's responsibilities were thrust upon her because of a weakness and apathy in the people around her. In her heart, I think her roles as a wife and mother came first.

In 1980 and 1981, our family lived in Chattanooga, Tennessee. This was during a period when efforts were underway to try to defeat the Equal Rights Amendment, and a woman who worshiped at the same congregation where we worshiped was involved in a big way. I still smile at the memory of calling her home one day to ask her something. Her husband answered the phone and said, "She's not home right now. In fact, she is *never* here anymore. She's out working for that group that thinks women ought to stay home!"

I do not believe Deborah was that way. I think her home responsibilities were what meant the most to her.

Can a Christian woman in the 21st century fulfill the role God intended and still work outside the home? What special challenges does she face if she does so?

_____

_____

_____

BACKGROUND

While not a great deal is known about Deborah, there is even less information on her husband. Basically, all we know is that his name was Lapidoth.

The period of time when Lapidoth and Deborah lived, however, is well-documented. At times, the book of Judges almost seems like a broken record because God's people kept repeating the same behaviors. The pattern was this: they would do evil and fall away from God, so He would allow them to be delivered into the hands of their enemies. Then, in the midst of oppression, they would repent and turn back to God, and He would send a deliverer. After that they would enjoy prosperity for a while, but without fail the cycle would start all over again.

When the story of Deborah begins in Judges 4, God has allowed Jabin, the king of Canaan, to oppress the Israelites. His dominion over them lasted for roughly 20 years. From all indications, the children of Israel were very intimidated by the Canaanites. It reminds me of the way they felt about the Philistines in the time of David. Jabin's army, led by a captain named Sisera, may not have had a giant, but they had something equally impressive: 900 chariots of iron. (Israel, on the other hand, probably did not even have chariots, much less chariots of iron!) Bible scholars tell us that those chariots were probably not made completely of iron, but rather were shod with iron or had iron scythes protecting them on either side of the axle. Such blades, of course, could easily cut down soldiers on foot. Israel's problem—not unlike ours today—was that they were overwhelmed by what was *seen*, and unfortunately tended to forget what was unseen (2 Corinthians 4:18, KJV).

Can you pinpoint any negative cycles you tend to repeat in your spiritual life? How can you break the chain?

_____

_____

_____

_____

LESSONS FROM DEBORAH

(1) Deborah was a woman of action. While all the men of Israel were cowering in fear, the Bible tells us that she **arose** (Judges 5:7). She was tired of her people being oppressed; she had endured enough. If no one else would do anything, then she would.

Too many times today I think we are guilty of sitting back, waiting on other people to take action. When that is the case, it is so easy to become negative and critical.

I love the old story about Mrs. Brown and Mrs. Smith, both members of the same church, who had gotten together one day to visit. Each of them had brought along a pair of their husbands trousers to mend as they talked.

"My husband is just so discouraged with the way things go at church," Mrs. Brown said. "Sometimes he says he just feels like quitting!"

"Really?" replied Mrs. Smith, surprised. "Why, my husband is just the opposite. He's excited about the work and finds more to do than he can ever get done."

There followed a brief silence while Mrs. Brown continued to patch the *seat* of her husband's pants, and Mrs. Smith patched the *knees* of the pants belonging to her mate.

Are you a doer or a talker? List some specific actions you can take to fill needs you see in your congregation and your community.

_____

_____

_____

(2) Deborah was a woman of courage. In Judges 4:6, we are introduced to a secondary character in the story of Deborah, a man by the name of Barak. Deborah summoned him from his home in Kedesh, and together they worked out a military strategy. It is evident from scripture that Deborah was not at all afraid of Sisera, the commander of Jabin's army. She told Barak to go toward Mt. Tabor and take 10,000 men from the children of Naphtali and Zebulun. Barak responded with one of the most unusual passages in the Bible ever spoken by a man to a woman. He said, basically, "I'll go—*if you go with me!*" What was it about this little housewife from Mt. Ephraim that made General Barak want her at his side? She had confidence, and it was contagious. It made him feel braver with her along.

Do we have that kind of effect on people? Is it easier for them to serve God when we are around? It should be.

(3) Deborah was a woman of praise. Judges 5 is a song of celebration because of what God did for His people. Deborah did not take any credit for the end results; she knew the victory belonged to the Lord. (She also refused to let Barak take any credit either, prophesying in Judges 4:9 that God would deliver Sisera into the hands of a woman.)

It is fascinating to me to see the different things God used to win battles in the Old Testament. With David (1 Samuel 17), He used a slingshot. With Gideon (Judges 7), He used pitchers, lanterns, and trumpets. In the story of Deborah and Barak, He used nature. We learn directly from the historian Josephus and indirectly from the song of Deborah that a storm of sleet and hail burst over the plain from the east, driving right into the face of Sisera and his men. The archers were ineffective because of the beating rain, and the swordsmen were handicapped by the biting cold.

Deborah and Barak, on the other hand, had the storm ahead of them, so they were not hurt by it. As they saw it hit, they continued on, their courage strengthened by the evidence of God's providential care. Flood waters raced down the Kishon River. It rained so hard that Sisera's celebrated iron chariots sank in the mud, and, as the weighty chariots stalled, other chariots ran into them. In all the confusion, many of the soldiers were killed.

Is it easier for people to serve God when we are around? It should be.

Sisera then left his chariot and ran for his life, finding haven (or so he thought!) in the tent of Jael, wife of Heber the Kenite. Jael coaxed him to sleep with an offering of warm milk, and while he napped took a tent peg and drove it through his temple. Thus, Deborah's prophesy was fulfilled. Sisera was delivered into the hands of a woman, Jabin's army was utterly destroyed, and the land had rest for forty years.

A SECOND EXAMPLE

Another woman in scripture who let God's light shine through her was Anna. We read her story in Luke 2:36-38.

Anna is one of the few people I can think of in the Bible whose name is a palindrome (spelled the same frontwards and backwards). But she is remarkable for much more than just that.

In her book, *Her Name Is Woman*, Gien Kaarssen describes Anna as "a woman who wasn't destroyed by a broken heart." That is an apt description, especially considering the time period when she lived. In those days, a woman's only identity was through her husband. (This is still the case today in some Middle Eastern countries.) The only thing a childless woman could do in Anna's day was return to her parent's home and wait for either a second husband or death.

Anna had every reason to despair, but she didn't.

Anna, however, found a third option. Like Hannah in the Old Testament, who gave her son to God (1 Samuel 1), Anna gave her own self to God and devoted her life to serving Him in the temple. (Interestingly enough, the name *Anna* in Greek is the same as *Hannah* in Hebrew.)

Anna was a woman who had every reason to despair, but she did not. She believed that God is near to the brokenhearted (Psalm 34:18), and she survived by staying near to Him.

NOT A GRUMPY OLD WOMAN

The name "Anna" means gracious. My mother-in-law used to tell a story about growing up in North Carolina as the youngest of nine children. She had seven sisters, two of whom were named Mabel and Grace. The family did not attend church regularly at the time. One summer, her daddy had hired some men to help him in the tobacco fields, and Mrs. Copeland remembers hearing one of them in the barn late one afternoon. He was singing "Amazing Grace." She had never heard the hymn before and asked her mama why the hired hand was singing about Mabel and Grace!

We know all about the amazing grace of God, don't we? To be gracious means, to a certain extent, to be God-like. Here are some further definitions: agreeable; marked by kindness and courtesy; characterized by charm and generosity of spirit.

According to the text, Anna was an old woman. Probably she was 84; although, some commentators think the reference means she had been a widow for 84 years. If they are right, then she was well over 100.

Do the definitions for someone who is gracious describe the elderly people you know? Maybe. But then again, maybe not. Many times when people reach advanced years, they develop a sour outlook on life.

Now I realize that many senior citizens struggle with painful health problems. But old age should never be considered a free license for negativity. Consider the following poem:

> Grandpa's right leg hurt him and the doctor said, "Old age."
> Grandpa, in a quandary, felt a sudden twinge of rage.
> "I think you are mistaken," he declared in accents bold.
> "My left leg doesn't hurt at all, and it is just as old!"

There are some people in the world (and not just old folks) you do not dare ask how they are doing because they might tell you—and tell you and tell you and tell you! I don't think Anna was that way. She did not feel sorry for herself.

> *Sometimes we tend to think what has happened to us is the worst thing ever.*

That reminds me of the old joke about a man who died in a flood and went to heaven. When it came time for Show and Tell, he wanted to tell the story about the big disaster in his hometown that had claimed his life, but Peter would not let him. He begged and begged until finally Peter relented. "Just remember, though," he cautioned, "Noah will be in the audience, and it will take a pretty good flood story to impress him!"

Sometimes we tend to think that what has happened to us is the worst thing ever, but all we have to do is look around, and we will see someone who has experienced something even more difficult. I imagine that is what Anna did. She did not have a pity party for herself and think she was the only person in the world who had ever suffered. She realized others were in pain, too, and she reached out to help them based on what she had learned through her own grief (2 Corinthians 1:3,4).

LESSONS FROM ANNA

(1) Anna was faithful. Luke 2:37 says she departed not from the temple. Is this to be taken literally? We cannot be absolutely sure. Some say it is very possible that, because of her age and her devotion, she actually had lodgings in the courts. Others think this merely implies that she was constantly there when any good work was to be done (or as we would say today, "every time the doors were opened"). Regardless of which one was true, she obviously lived a life where spiritual things held priority.

Verse 37 also says that she fasted and prayed day and night. Despite her advanced years, she kept the customary feasts that were twice a week. Moses had appointed one yearly fast (the day of Atonement), but apparently the Pharisees had introduced the custom of fasting twice a week, on Mondays and Thursdays, to commemorate the days when

Moses supposedly ascended and descended Mt. Sinai. Anna also must have spent an unusual amount of time in prayer, above and beyond the recognized hours of prayer at that time (9 a.m. and 3 p.m.).

(2) Because of Anna's devotion to God, He honored her with a great privilege. Anna was able to see the baby Jesus at the ceremonial service of His mother's purification, 40 days after His birth.

What if she had not been constantly in the temple? Just think, she might have missed this greatest of events.

It is said that King Oscar of Sweden once visited a church in the Netherlands, arriving (as he desired) without any fanfare. He chose a particular pew and sat down, only to have the lady who normally sat there walk up and inform him that was *her* seat! Later on, when the woman learned that it was royalty she had booted out of the way, she was mortified. "I didn't expect there to be a king present in worship!" she said.

We never know what we may miss out on if we are not present on the Lord's day. One thing we can be sure of, though: there will always be a King present!

(3) After Anna saw the young Messiah, she "spoke of Him to all" (Luke 2:38, NKJV).

I like this quote from Matthew Henry: "Those that have an acquaintance with Christ themselves should do all they can to make others acquainted with Him." That is what Anna did, and that is exactly what we should do.

> What do you do that is "above and beyond" what is required? What blessings come about as a result of being constantly about our Father's business?
>
> _____
>
> _____
>
> _____
>
> _____
>
> _____
>
> _____

SUMMARY

The Bible is filled with people who let their lights shine (Matthew 5:16) to the people around them. Two of these are Deborah in the Old Testament and Anna in the New Testament.

From these women, we learn that God can use anyone in His service, as long as that person allows himself to be used by God.

CHAPTER 12

Making a Difference:

Modern-Day Reflectors

Tops of bookshelves in my living room are lined with family photographs. There is one of my husband at age four (yes, he had that mischievous grin even then), various senior year portraits of our children, candid groupings of cousins, even an old black-and-white of my sister and me, circa 1958.

The other day, as I dusted the photos—something I only do on rare occasions!—I paused to examine the most recent addition. It is an 8 by 10 color reprint of a shot that appeared in our local newspaper last year during basketball season. The photograph shows our son Luke, a player for the University of North Alabama, bringing the ball down court, closely guarded by an opponent from a West Florida team. Studying it closely, it dawned on me that here I have framed and prominently displayed in my home a large portrait of a total stranger, someone whose name I do not even know! I am sure he would be shocked to learn that his picture sits on my shelf.

That started me to thinking. Are there people who, figuratively, have a spot on my life's shelf, who have been an influence on me, but may not be aware of it? Probably there are. And it is just as possible that I may have influenced someone without my ever having known.

> *It is possible I may have influenced someone without my ever having known.*

There is a sweet poem by Brod Bagert in a juvenile book entitled *Giant Children*. It says:

> Psst! Listen very closely,
> There's something you should know.
> It's all about a giant school
> Where Giant Children Go
>
> Pages turn at giant speed
> As giant children learn to read.
> And giant brains are really quick
> When working on arithmetic.

They pound the beat on giant drums
And finger paint with giant thumbs,
Sing giant songs with giant lips
And boogie-dance with giant hips.

Giant shoes on giant feet
And giant giggles when they meet.
I watch them hour after hour,
Giant kids with giant power.

I'm just the classroom hamster
But I promise you it's true —
This is the school where giants go,
And the giant kids are YOU.

The point is, if you are a hamster, even grade-school children can appear to be giants.

As Christians, we should realize that people are watching us, and we have an opportunity to be "giants" in their eyes because of the things we do. We can have a significant influence on others if we will strive to reflect God's light.

In this chapter, we will look at some modern-day examples of people who have done this very thing.

CATHERINE LAWES

In one of the *Chicken Soup for the Soul* books, Tim Kimmel shares the story of Lewis Lawes, who became the warden at Sing Sing Prison in 1921. At the time, Sing Sing was a rough place, but by the time Lawes retired twenty years later, there had been quite a turnaround. When asked about the changes that had taken place, Lawes gave all the credit to his wife Catherine.

When her husband first became warden, everyone warned Catherine––then a young wife with three small children—to stay away from Sing Sing. But she paid them no heed. At the first prison basketball game, she and her kids walked right in and sat in the stands among the inmates!

She was determined to get to know the men on an individual basis. When she found out that one convicted murderer was blind, she taught him to read Braille. She learned sign language so that she could communicate with another prisoner who was deaf-mute.

In 1937, Catherine Lawes was killed in a car accident. Her body was laid out for viewing at the Lawes home, which was only three-quarters of a mile down the road from the prison.

According to Kimmel, on the day of the visitation, the acting warden, filling in for Lewis Lawes, took an early morning walk around the grounds.

> [H]e was shocked to see a large crowd of the toughest, hardest-looking criminals gathered like a herd of animals at the main gate. He came closer and noted tears of grief and sadness. He knew how much they loved Catherine. He turned and faced the men, "All right, men, you can go. Just be sure to check in tonight!" Then he opened the gate and a parade of criminals walked, without a guard, the three-quarters of a mile to stand in line to pay their final respects to Catherine Lawes. And every one of them checked back in. Every one!

Catherine Lawes was buried right outside the prison walls.

> What prejudices did Catherine have to overcome to involve herself in the lives of the inmates?
>
> _____
> _____
> _____
> _____

LAURA BRADLEY

In a 1987 article in the *Chicago Tribune,* Bob Greene recorded the story of Douglas Maurer of Creve Coeur, Missouri—a young man who was diagnosed with leukemia at fifteen.

Hospitalized for the first time and facing at least three years of chemotherapy, Maurer was understandably frightened. His aunt called a St. Louis florist and ordered some flowers, hoping to brighten his spirits. According to Greene, the salesclerk who answered the phone sounded so young that the aunt was worried she would not understand the significance of the arrangement. "I want the planter especially attractive," she specified. "It's for my teenage nephew who has leukemia."

When the flowers arrived at the hospital, Maurer opened the envelope. Along with his aunt's card, another card was included. It read:

> Douglas—I took your order. I work at Brix Florist. I had
> leukemia when I was seven years old. I'm 22 years old
> now. Good luck. My heart goes out to you.
> > Sincerely,
> > Laura Bradley

For the first time since becoming ill, Douglas felt a ray of hope.

Later, when contacted by Greene, Laura Bradley explained that she had slipped the card into the envelope without telling anyone. She had not been at the florist very long and was afraid she might get in trouble, but hearing of Douglas' diagnosis had reminded her of the time she had been told she had leukemia. "I realized what the boy must be going through. I wanted him to know that you really *can* get better."

"My heart goes out to you."

Greene wrote:

> It's funny; Douglas Maurer was in a hospital filled with
> millions of dollars of the most sophisticated medical
> equipment. He was being treated by expert doctors
> and nurses with medical training totaling hundreds
> of years. But it was a salesclerk in a flower shop, a
> woman making $170 a week, who—by taking the
> time to care, and by being willing to go with what
> her heart told her to do—gave Douglas hope and the
> will to carry on.

MAK SHULIST

Young Mak Shulist passed away on April 8, 2004 from an inoperable brain tumor. But an article in the Florence, Alabama *Times-Daily,* reported the following Tuesday that the nine-year-old's dying wish will benefit his friends for a long time to come.

Instead of asking for a trip to Disney World or a meeting with someone famous—the most typical favors sought by terminally ill youngsters––Shulist requested that the Make-A-Wish Foundation construct a seven-foot rock-climbing wall on the playground of his elementary school.

"It says a lot about the family and the type of person he was—selfless, thoughtful, and caring," commented the principal of the school, Dave Knes.

"We learned a lesson from a nine-year-old—that even when we're going through tough times we should be thinking of other people and not ourselves."

Shulist had last attended his school in Ellisville, Missouri the previous fall. He had been sick about a year.

The wall was completed just in time for the youngster to view a video tape of his classmates on it before he passed away.

Have you ever done anything as unselfish as Mak did? How do you think he had been influenced by his family members? What kind of influence, in turn, do you think he had on them?

_____

_____

_____

RYAN HRELJAC

In January of 1998, a first-grade teacher at a private school in Kemptville, Ontario talked with the students in her class about living conditions in Africa. A little six-year-old boy named Ryan Hreljac was touched when he learned how many children on that continent die each year as a result of drinking contaminated water. Ryan went home from school and told his parents that he needed $70 to buy a well.

Susan and Mark Hreljac did not pay much attention to Ryan's request at first. But when he refused to let the subject die, they sat him down and explained that he was talking about a lot of money. "If you are really serious about raising $70, you can do extra chores," his mom suggested, thinking that would end the discussion once and for all.

But Ryan surprised her. He washed windows, vacuumed the house and picked up pine cones, saving the money he earned in an old cookie jar. As the dollars accumulated, Susan Hreljac contacted WaterCan, a non-profit organization in Ottawa, Ontario. That April, Ryan presented his $70 to the agency's executive director, Nicole Bosley. Bosley thanked him, but she explained that while $70 would fund a hand pump, the figure for actually drilling a well was actually closer to $2,000.

Ryan was undaunted. "I'll just do more chores," he said.

A friend of Susan Hreljac's, Brenda Cameron Couch, e-mailed family and friends about Ryan's project, encouraging them to help. The Canadian International Development Agency agreed to match two-for-one all funds that were raised.

When Ryan had topped the $700 mark, he and his mom were invited to meet Gizaw Shibru, the director for Uganda at Canadian Physicians for Aid and Relief. In talking with Ryan, Shibru mentioned that drilling equipment would make possible more wells. So Ryan set his sights on a new goal: $25,000 to buy a small drill.

Derek Puddicombe, a journalist for the Ottawa *Citizen* and an old friend of Susan's wrote an article about Ryan that was reprinted in newspapers all across Canada. The money poured in.

Ryan's teacher (he was now in the second grade) set up a pen-pal program with children in her class and children in Angolo Primary, a school in an area of northern Uganda that had benefited from Ryan's well.

In July of 2000, Ryan and his parents were able to travel to Angolo and meet the people in that village he had helped. Ryan was stunned that some 3,000 children all knew his name.

More than $70,000 has been raised for construction equipment on another continent, all because of a little Canadian schoolboy who still prays: "I wish for everyone in Africa to have clean water."

What examples can you think of from the Bible where only one person made a difference?

_____

_____

_____

_____

SUMMARY

The four examples given in this chapter all have something in common. They made a tremendous difference in the lives of those around them. They did it by being unselfish, generous, and spontaneous, and not letting what others thought or expected hold them back.

The fact that two of the ones cited were youngsters illustrates an important principle Jesus Himself reiterated: "unless you change and become like little children, you will never enter the kingdom of heaven" (Matthew 18:3).

CHAPTER 13

Increasing Our Wattage

Most of us who attended Sunday school as children probably remember very well holding up our index fingers and singing with gusto a song about brightening up our neighborhoods.

Well-known author Chuck Swindoll, however, questions the semantics of those age-old lyrics. "Where," he asks, "did we pick up the mistaken idea of 'This little light of mine, I'm gonna let it shine'?

"We are never called 'little lights' in the Bible . . . we are *stars*. Bold, blazing, light-giving stars! This aching, hurting, confused world of lost humanity exists in dark rooms without light. Let it shine, fellow star!"

> *We are never called "little lights" in the Bible.*

How can I go from having merely a "little" light to shining forth as brilliantly as the sun (Matthew 13:43)? How can I increase my wattage?

This chapter will examine various ways to become a brighter beacon for the Lord.

Penetrate and Permeate

In Matthew 5, Jesus talked about the kind of relationship we are supposed to have with people in the world around us. Contrary to what some may think, Christians are not to isolate themselves, but are rather expected—required, if you will—to mix, mingle, and make their presence known.

To illustrate the type of interaction that is to take place, Jesus used the examples of salt and light. Think for a minute about what those two things have in common. Both are known for having an impact, are they not? Add salt to food and a notable improvement occurs. Light one little candle in a darkened room, and the difference is very evident.

Several years ago, Roger and I spent the night with an acquaintance in another state. Our hostess, a sweet widow who lived alone, really gave us the red carpet treatment and insisted that we stay in her bedroom for the night. The only problem: she was a smoker, and we were not at all used to the smells such a habit incurs.

A couple of days later, back at home, as I unpacked our suitcase, I noticed that every item of clothing I removed from our suitcase had the unmistakable odor of cigarettes. The smell had penetrated and permeated each object with which it had come in contact.

> *Light one candle in a darkened room, and the difference is very evident.*

That is the kind of impact we as Christians are to have on the world around us. We are to invade it, take it over, and spread our influence throughout it completely.

Do we do that? Not always. In fact, there are times when our illumination—or lack of it—can be compared to an incident that occurred a few years back in Pennsylvania. Six lives were lost when a small, private plane crashed into a mountain. The tragedy occurred near a 68-foot stainless steel cross that served as a marker for a Methodist training center. Reporting the tragedy, the Associated Press dispatch said, "The cross has electric lights which could have shown the way, but they were not turned on at the time."

SHOW AND TELL

In one of my favorite *Peanuts* comic strips, Lucy comes up to her brother Linus and tells him that she has converted someone in her class to her way of religious thinking. Knowing his sister, Linus can hardly believe his ears. "How did you do that?" he asked.

Lucy explained, "I told him everything I believe and asked him if he believed it, too. When we came to something he didn't see my way, I just hit him over the head with my lunch box until he believed it."

For too long, I think, we have tried to "hit people over the head" with our beliefs, expecting them to fall right into line with us. Unfortunately, it does not work that way. Telling needs to be accompanied by—or better yet, preceded by—showing. This is evidenced so well in the life of Ezra. In Ezra 7:10, we read that he had "prepared his heart to seek the law of the Lord, and to **do it** (emphasis mine), and to teach. . . " (KJV).

Doing what the law of the Lord says—living it out for others to see––is one of the greatest teaching methods there is. Peter was talking about

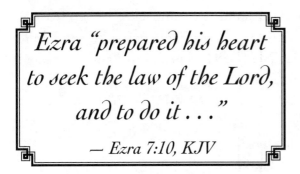

> *Ezra "prepared his heart to seek the law of the Lord, and to do it . . ."*
>
> — *Ezra 7:10, KJV*

this very thing in 1 Peter 3:1 when he said that non-believing husbands could sometimes be won "without talk by the behavior of their wives."

In *The Message*, Eugene Petersen says, "Our work as God's servants gets validated—or not—in the details" (2 Corinthians 6:4).

Let's look now at some of those details—specific behaviors that will show Christ to others.

(1) Being kind. How do we treat those around us? Are we disagreeable and unpleasant? You may remember an impressive woman in the Old Testament by the name of Abigail. According to 1 Samuel 25, her not-so-impressive husband was one of the biggest grouches around. Nabal was a Calebite, which literally means *a dog*, and apparently that is the personality he had—surly, snappish, and always snarling. The Bible says he was so ill-natured that no one dared talk to him (1 Samuel 25:17)! His wife, on the other hand, was considerate, helpful, and peace-loving. In our treatment of others, we should strive to be like Abigail, and not Nabal, always conscious of the impression we may leave.

Showing kindness is an indication to the world that Jesus reigns in our lives. I have been told that at Buckingham Palace in London, Queen Elizabeth's standard that flies over the residence is a sign to the world that she is there. (I have also heard—but do not know if this is true—that when Dolly Parton is in Dollywood, one of her bras is raised up the flag pole to let people know she is in town!) Kindness exhibited in the life of a Christian is a sign to the world that Jesus is present in our hearts.

Think about some of the strangers whose paths have crossed yours in recent days. What kind of impression did you make on them? How can you improve your kindness quotient?

_____

_____

_____

Our oldest son lives in San Antonio, Texas, where he works as a youth minister. San Antonio, of course, is famous for the Alamo, and that is where Adam always takes visitors who come to see him. On a wall near the main entrance to the Alamo are numerous portraits of men who lost their lives there. Among them is a portrait that bears the following inscription: *James Butler Bonham—No picture of him exists. This portrait is of his nephew, Major James Bonham, who greatly resembled his uncle.*

No literal portrait exists of Jesus either; He is not here on the earth anymore for people to see what He is like. But, hopefully, the actions of His followers "greatly resemble" His, so non-Christians, by looking at Christians, can know what Jesus was like. Kindness can make a favorable impression for the Lord and can even be a tool for evangelism.

(2) Loving the unlovable. Someone has said, "Everybody loves a kitten, but nobody pets a porcupine." It is easy to love those who are loveable, those who will return your affection. But Jesus said, "If you love those who love you, what reward will you get? Are not even the tax collectors doing that?" (Matthew 5:46).

> *"If you love those who love you, what reward will you get? Are not even the tax collectors doing that?"*
> — *Matthew 5:46*

The names of those Jesus befriended on earth read like a veritable list of the most *un*wanted. (Think: outcasts, rejects, those socially unacceptable.) In contrast, consider your own "inner circle." The majority of us, I am afraid, spend the bulk of our time with people who are just like us. But as Christ's followers, we are called upon to go beyond that. We should love those who act like they do not want it. (Truth is, they probably want it, and need it, as much as anyone.)

(3) Becoming vulnerable. This means we quit worrying about ourselves, how we look, how we come across to others, or what kind of response we will get. The emphasis shifts from self to others.

As he left the clubhouse, having just won a tournament, Argentine golfer Robert De Vincenzo was approached by a young woman who

152 ✽ *Holes In The Darkness*

congratulated him for the victory and proceeded to ask him to assist her in paying for medical treatments for her sick child. De Vincenzo very graciously endorsed the check he had just received and gave her all of his winnings.

The next week, as he lunched in the country club, an official from the Golf Association told him that it had been discovered that the woman was a fraud. She had no baby and was not even married, as it turned out.

De Vincenzo replied, "You mean there is no baby who is dying? That is the best news I have heard all week."

When we let our lights shine, others may take advantage of us, but that is all right. What really matters is that we are going to do the right thing.

THE UNIQUE GARNET

The birthstone for those born in January is a reddish-brown gemstone called a garnet. Interestingly, the garnet has a rich history. Tradition tells us that ancient kings made it the centerpiece of their breastplates. Some historians even claim that Noah placed one on the bow of the ark!

Just what made the garnet so special? In olden times, many believed that while other stones merely reflect light, the garnet generated illumination from within. Because of that, it was sometimes referred to as the "third eye."

Before electricity was discovered, the garnet was coveted in times of emergency. When everything around was pitch dark, people thought a garnet beamed forth an inner light.

Scientists today, of course, label such beliefs mere superstition. Still, I think the myth illustrates a very valid point. Most people in the world today are merely reflectors. Treated well, they respond with smiles and

Think of an incident when you reflected the same type of attitude you encountered. Then think of a time when someone responded to you with an action better than your own.

_____

_____

_____

gracious words. But dealt with a bit of ungraciousness or lack of courtesy, they respond accordingly.

What about us? Do we reflect what we encounter? What happens when we come in contact with a rude clerk, an incompetent waiter, or an inconsiderate driver? How do we react?

Here is an idea that I have used sometimes to help me avoid being merely a reflector.

If you have ever had a toothache—and most of us have at one time or another—you know just how painful that can be. It really makes you hurt all over. Let's suppose I go into a store one day, and someone there is really rude to me, a clerk or another customer or a driver I meet in the parking lot. In my mind, whenever that happens, I just tell myself, "Oh, I guess he (or she) has a toothache today. I understand how lousy that makes you feel." Thinking along these lines helps me to be understanding and sympathetic and respond in a civil manner. (Note: To make the preceding approach more applicable to you personally, substitute the idea of a toothache with arthritis, hemorrhoids, migraines, or any other physical ailment with which you can genuinely relate.)

THE HOUSE AS WELL AS THE HILL

In the Matthew 5 passage referred to earlier, where Jesus gave the illustration of salt and light, it is important to note that the reference to light is two-fold. Notice:

"You are the light of the world. A city on a hill cannot be hidden. Neither do people light a lamp and put it under a bowl. Instead they put it on its stand, and it gives light to everyone in the house" (verses 14,15).

Someone pointed out to me once that this passage underscores the necessity of being a light not only to those out in the world, but also to those right in our household. In other words, it will do no good to be a "city on a hill" if our own household remains in darkness.

> *This passage underscores the necessity of being a light not only to those out in the world, but also to those right in our households.*

This is an important point to remember as we think about increasing our wattage. Nowhere should our light shine more brightly than in our homes. Unfortunately, however, it seems that sometimes we are more patient and loving with others than we are with members of our own families.

Joyce Landorf, in her book *Changepoints*, tells about visiting in the Sunday school department of her church one day. Just by observing for a few minutes, she said she could tell if the teacher had a child of her own in the class. How was that? "Her sweet, patient, gentle instructions and teaching went to all children but one. To that child, she almost snarled, *Be still! Be quiet!* The teacher demanded instant obedience and mature perfection from her own child when she would never dream of asking for it so bluntly from others!"

I love a story told about a man and woman who had never met before, but found themselves assigned to the same sleeping room on a transcontinental train. After the initial embarrassment and uneasiness, they both stretched out on their bunks and went to sleep, the man in the upper berth and the woman in the lower berth.

In the middle of the night, the man leaned over, awakened the woman and said, "I'm so sorry to bother you, but I'm awfully cold. I was wondering if you could possibly reach over and hand me another blanket."

The woman leaned out and with a glint in her eye said, "I have a better idea. Just for tonight, let's pretend that we are married."

"Alright!" the man replied, shocked but pleased.

The woman then rolled back over and said, "Get your own blanket."

Is that how we treat our mates? We smile at such a silly story, but I am afraid there may be a kernel of truth in it. Sometimes we do not show our spouse the basic courtesy we would give a total stranger.

Have you ever been in the middle of a disagreement with your husband, perhaps a bit heated, when the phone rings? Do you use the same tone of voice when you answer the phone that you have just been using with your mate? Probably not. We reserve our gruffest, most cutting inflections for those we love the most! (An interesting sidelight: it has been said that 90 percent of the friction of daily life is caused by the wrong tone of voice.)

As God's people, we need to exhibit His love to *everyone*—beginning with our own families. And, when we have developed good, strong, healthy relationships with our spouses and children, then (and only then) will we be ready to let our lights shine to others.

> How do you treat those closest to you? What improvements can and should you make?
>
> _____
>
> _____
>
> _____
>
> _____

SUMMARY

Leo Tolstoy once wrote, "The business of a Christian . . . is everywhere and always one: to increase one's fire and let it give light to men."

Increasing one's fire means becoming, as Jesus indicated in Matthew 5, salt and light. In other words, God's people need to penetrate and permeate their surroundings and have an impact on those around them.

Some of the ways we can better do this involves being kind, loving the unlovable and allowing ourselves to become vulnerable.

An important point to remember is that not only does God expect our lights to shine to those who are outsiders, He also expects them to shine to those who are "in the house" (Matthew 5:15). Increasing our wattage should begin with the relationship we have with our family members.

BIBLIOGRAPHY

Chapter 1:

Dobson, James. *Stories of the Heart and Home.* Nashville: Word Publishing, 2000, pp. 13-15.

Chapter 2:

Coffman, James Burton. *Commentary on James, 1 & 2 Peter, 1, 2, & 3 John, Jude.* Austin, Texas: Firm Foundation Publishing House, 1979, p. 378.

Chapter 3:

Spurgeon, Charles Haddon. *Psalms.* Edited by David Otis Fuller. (Formerly published under the title *The Treasury of David* in two volumes.) Grand Rapids, Michigan: Kregel Publications, 1968, p. 510.

Clarke, Adam. *Commentary on the Holy Bible.* Abridged from the original six-volume work by Ralph Earle. Grand Rapids, Michigan: Baker Book House, 1967, p. 523.

Dobson, *Stories of the Heart and Home,* p. 4.

Chapter 4:

Brand, Dr. Paul and Philip Yancey. *In His Image.* Grand Rapids, Michigan: Zondervan Publishing House, 1984, pp. 17,18.

Barclay, William. *The Gospel of John, Vol. 1, Chapters 1-7.* (Revised edition.) Philadelphia: The Westminster Press, 1975, pp. 123,124.

Barclay, William. *The Gospel of John, Vol. 2, Chapters 8-21,* p. 263.

Cook, F.C. *The Bible Commentary, Vol. IX, Romans to Philemon.* Grand Rapids, Michigan: Baker Book House, p. 552.

Chapter 5:

Wiersbe, Warren W. *Be Real.* Wheaton, Illinois: Victor Books, A division of SP Publications, Inc., 1972, p. 25.

Taylor, Kenneth. *Living Psalms and Proverbs With the Major Prophets*. Wheaton, Illinois: Tyndale House Publications, 1967.

Chapter 6:

Allen, Charles L. *You Are Never Alone*. Old Tappan, New Jersey: Fleming H. Revell Company, pp. 15,16.

Coffman, James Burton. *Commentary on Genesis*. Abilene, Texas: ACU Press, 1985, p. 93.

Murrah, Roger and Randy Van Warner, *"I'm In a Hurry,"* American Pride, 1992.

Atchley, Rick. *Sinai Summit: Meeting God With Our Character Crisis*. Fort Worth, Texas: Sweet Publishing, 1993, pp. 85,86.

Chapter 7:

Henry, Matthew. *Commentary on the Whole Bible*. Grand Rapids, Michigan: Zondervan Publishing House, 1960, p. 380.

Coffman, James Burton. *Commentary on First Kings*. Abilene, Texas: Abilene Christian University Press, 1993, pp. 168,169,171.

Cook, F.C. *The Bible Commentary, Volume II, Joshua to 1 Kings*. Grand Rapids, Michigan: Baker Book House, pp. 564,566.

Chapter 8:

Rose, Lyn. *Mom's Diary*. West Monroe, Louisiana: Howard Publishing Company, 1994, p. 119.

Portnoy, Gary and Judy Hart Angelo, *"Where Everybody Knows Your Name,"* Addax Music Co., Inc. (ASCAP), 1982.

Copeland, Teddy. *Playing the Hand You Are Dealt*. Florence, Alabama: Lambert Book House.

Chapter 9:

Higgs, Liz Curtis. *Really Bad Girls of the Bible*. Waterville, Maine: Thorndike Press, 2000, p. 423.

Lucado, Max. *In the Grip of Grace*. Word Publishing, 1996, p. 93.

Chapter 10:

Canfield, Jack, Mark Victor Hansen, Jennifer Read Hawthorne and Marci Shimoff. *Chicken Soup for the Mother's Soul.* Deerfield Beach, Florida: Health Communications, Inc., 1997. "Moving Mountains," by Jim Stovall, pp. 94,95.

Keller, Phillip. *A Shepherd Looks At Psalms 23.* Grand Rapids, Michigan: Zondervan Publishing House. 1970, pp. 51,52.

Chapter 11:

Kaarssen, Gien. *Her Name Is Woman.* Colorado Springs, Colorado: NavPress, 1975, pp. 149,150.

Henry, Matthew, p. 1419.

Chapter 12:

Bagert, Brod. *Giant Children.* New York: Scholastic, Inc., 2002.

Canfield, Jack, Mark Victor Hansen, Hanoch McCarty and Meladee McCarty. *A Fourth Course of Chicken Soup for the Soul.* Deerfield Beach, Florida: Health Communications, Inc., 1997. "Changed Lives," by Tim Kimmel, pp. 60,61.

Greene, Bob. "My Heart Goes Out to You," *Reader's Digest,* condensed from *Chicago Tribune,* July 6, 1987.

Cook, Kathy. "Ryan's Well," *Canadian Reader's Digest,* January 2001.

Chapter 13:

Swindoll, Charles R. *Laugh Again.* Nashville, Tennessee: W Publishing Group, 1992, p. 101.

Petersen, Eugene. *The Message.* Colorado Springs, Colorado: Nav Press, 1993.

Landorf, Joyce. *Changepoints.* Balcony Publishing, Inc., 1992.

Notes

Notes